NOTES FROM THE ROOM

Your Guide to the Art of Acting & Show Business

CHRIS CLAVELLI

Edited by Shami J. McCormick

THE Joy Press
Los Angeles

NOTES FROM THE ROOM

© 2024 by Chris Clavelli

ALL RIGHTS RESERVED. No part of this publication may be reproduced, distributed or transmitted in any form or by any means, including photocopying, recording, or other electronic or mechanical methods, without the prior written permission of the author or publisher, except in the case of brief quotations embodied in critical reviews and certain other noncommercial uses permitted by copyright law. For permission requests, contact the author at cclavelli1161@gmail.com.

ISBN # 978-0-9727450-5-5

THE Joy Press
Los Angeles

For Jessy—
the best damn actor I ever knew.

The creative adult is the child who survived.

FOREWORD

CHRIS CLAVELLI IS ONTO SOMETHING.

He has thought a lot about this and his decades in the business—with all of their knocks and joys—have led him to some very clear and articulate thinking about what it means to be an actor and what it *takes* to be an actor.

And he is deadly serious, even though he shares his thoughts with great compassion and humor.

What he says about what we actors do aligns completely with my own views. I tell my students that I don't think acting is mysterious at all. The effect of it, however, is completely magical.

All it is, is *very, very good pretending*.

At five, we're all geniuses at it playing in the sandbox. We are alive in the moment and our imaginations are operating at a hundred and fifty percent. You don't for a minute actually *believe* you are the King or Queen of England. You haven't had a psychotic break. You know you're playing, but you are *alive* in this reality you've created. And when your sister jumps in the sandbox and says, "There's a monster coming!" you don't say, "I'm going to need a few minutes to think about that." You instantly go along with the story.

And Chris is right. Someone along the way tells us to stop

showing off or calm down and we become self-conscious and aware, and all that freedom of play dries up.

The armor is firmly in place. And, by the way, it's completely necessary for us all to exist in the world. But it is death to being an actor.

Any acting teacher, with any protocol—Meisner, Strasberg, Hagen, Adler, or Joe Blow—is simply looking for a way to help you find that freedom again. But there is not one *right way* to get there. Don't believe Svengali when he shouts that he alone knows the secret to being a great actor! Whatever you find that helps you live without the fear of being shamed or failing in front of an audience will become the techniques that are valuable to *you*.

But in this book, Chris has a wonderful way of helping you find those techniques for yourself. He speaks beautifully about the nobility of what we do, its "essentialness", and then peppers those thoughts with simple tips: *Don't move on a laugh.*

Young actors don't always know the power of stillness onstage. The great actress, Geraldine Page, who was beyond astonishing, was sometimes known for being a fussy actress. While rehearsing one of her great triumphs, *The Rainmaker*, director Joseph Anthony shouted at her from the audience, "Gerry, don't just *do something: Stand there!*" It takes great courage to be still onstage, but it is often a great way into a character. Actors tend to be frightened of not doing something onstage. If you're at a loss in rehearsal, I have always found that by simply being still and removing the obligation to be busy, one is able to let all kinds of unexpected impulses arise. Sometimes just breathing onstage is remarkably compelling.

And Chris also identifies that our job as actors is to disappear in the story. I have come to think many actors, big stars even, don't completely understand what our job even is. Too much energy is spent trying to fill the "Unfillable Hole." Their egos are way too front and center. Their acting can be brilliant, but we as audience members can sense that they are asking for our approval more than turning the light on what it means to be alive. We can be dazzled by their somersaults, but we don't learn anything.

I always wondered why some of the stars from what we call "The Golden Age of Hollywood" impressed me more than their talented, modern-day equivalents. I have come to believe that the great stars who worked under the studio system, however brutal it could be, *knew* they were the stars of the movie and didn't need to spend any energy on that. The post-studio-system stars, who are all freelancers looking for work, seem to me to be spending an awful lot of the movie *proving* they deserve to be the lead. There's an awful lot of, "Look, Ma—I'M ACTING!" energy.

There is a breathtaking moment in Colin Higgins' wonderful film, *Harold and Maude*, where young, withdrawn Harold remarks to a joyous 80-year-old Maude, "You sure have a way with people..." to which she simply smiles and replies, "Well, they're my species."

Chris Clavelli knows about this, too. He understands to be a beautiful actor is to embrace that which makes us human: all the joy and sadness from which there is no escape. When we, as audience members, see that kind of authentic behavior onstage or in a film, we simply cannot look away. We recognize something about ourselves. We're not just killing time being entertained. We're actually learning about being alive, seeing someone else go through the same experiences we all must go through. At best, we are comforted knowing we are not alone as we see how others—even in a fictional setting—experience and deal with those things. We may not even be able to articulate it. However, to see an audience lost in being told a story, you know how mysterious and magical our work is.

Essential and noble indeed.

And it can be as easy as playing in the sandbox.

—Reed Birney, May 2023

PROLOGUE

NOTES: *a director's guide to an actor's performance. Traditionally given at the end of a rehearsal, a take or a performance. Shakespeare's Hamlet gave the first note in his advice to the players:*

"Speak the speech, I pray you, trippingly on the tongue…"

ROOM: *any space where art is created. A rehearsal hall, the soundstage of a major Hollywood studio, your childhood backyard full of autumn leaves.*

We are born actors. None of us needs to learn how to transform a pillow into a fort, a tablecloth into a cape, or believe we are something we are not: a fearsome dragon, a brave firefighter, a brilliant teacher, or even an elven king. 'Make believe' is our state of being. Indeed, we come into this world blessed with all the ingredients of an expressive artist. Where does that go?

Sadly, our culture of 'get it right, speak when spoken to, be a good boy, don't cry, stand still, wait your turn' beats it out of us. Moreover, our devices have drawn our eyes from wonder at the night's sky to a series of inanities—memes, TikToks, and

GIFs that are shorthand versions of human emotion. The fact that we seem to have all the answers at our fingertips has eliminated curiosity for curiosity's sake. Furthermore, with millions of facts readily available, we have become less certain about relying on our own critical thinking and imagination. We struggle to find the right question, let alone ask it. Having all the answers has taken all the fun out of life and made us terrified of doubt.

Our devices, as useful as they can sometimes be, have crushed the spirit of empathy. With our eyes down and not out, and our ears stuffed with buds, we have insulated ourselves against the very thing that is at the core of all great acting: intimate listening, active connection and spontaneous reaction. And, of course, the crushing effects of the pandemic lock-down and its aftermath did much to annihilate human interaction. Stuck in our rooms, we were all hungry for the joys of socializing. But for the actor, the pandemic meant not being able to play; not being able to be. It was akin to slow torture.

We may come by our emotional blocks honestly: fear of doubt, fear of turning off the screen, fear of emotional and physical interaction and engagement, and more. However, as actors, these blocks hinder us from creating rich characters deeply rooted in dynamic truth. What to do? First, as an actor, you live in doubt. Artistic doubt is the space between the answers; artistic maturity is the ability to live in that space for a long time—or at least until we find the impulse within us to act. This is true from audition through production and all the moments in between. We are going to look at this process and how to approach it. In the end, I hope you will have a strong foundation from which to navigate your career.

More of all this later in this book. For now, allow me to

take you back in time, when my acting was desperate for liberation and focus. You may identify. It was the spring of 1983.

In a classroom at Emerson College, I was playing George in Edward Albee's masterpiece *Who's Afraid of Virginia Wolf*. A part I was twenty-five years too young for and had no earthly business playing. Totally absurd. That fateful day, our professor was ill and a man named Sweeney took the class. That's all I remember of him. Sweeney: Hollywood couldn't have chosen a better moniker. After a miserable initial pass at the scene, Sweeney pulled each of us aside, gently laid a hand on our shoulders and whispered direction in our ears. The second pass was extraordinary. Sweeney had lifted the veil for us. I tasted the magic that day, and I've been chasing that high ever since. My mission in this book is to demystify the acting process and lift the veil for you, as Sweeney did for me in The Brimmer Street Theatre.

Though I now spend most of my life as a director and an educator, I still see the world as an actor. I know the fear and joy of it. As part of The Actors Studio Drama School, MFA program, I taught Acting Shakespeare to dozens of international students who spoke English as a second language. At first, I was mortified by the task but what they taught me was invaluable. In its essence, acting is storytelling. We must never forget why we loved those little books our parents read to us at bedtime, and remind ourselves that what a theatre or film audience is there to see—to hear—is a good old-fashioned tale. This book will address the components of acting that create rich stories and dynamic characterizations.

In addition to guiding you through a series of acting studies, *Notes From the Room* covers all aspects of an actor's life: the business, auditions, agents, casting directors, producers, theatre, film, TV, the players, rehearsal techniques, terminology and a process of finding a spirituality that supports your calling. By book's end, you will have a guide to the rest of your acting career and an approach to the art of being an actor.

NOTE:
To Be or Not to Be

Before we start, there comes a time, sometimes many times in your career, when you'll think about getting out of the business. It's a necessary debate; one which all but the lucky or independently wealthy have to have, as the stress of handling the everyday challenges of a career in entertainment can be debilitating to your soul as well as your bank account. These days, it's an even greater crisis because most of you transitioning out of college have racked up thousands of dollars in student debt. So, it's no wonder you'll fantasize about pulling up stakes, moving back to Ohio, buying a little home, getting a steady gig, and raising a family. And why not? What's the point of standing in line to sign up to audition for a role that pays so poorly it'll mean taking on another side job? With each audition and possible rejection, that cottage in Ohio looks better and better. In my thirty-five years as a professional actor, I threatened to quit dozens of times. Each time, my wife and friends would talk me down, and I'd return to my tribe. It's a growing pain. An extremely cynical teacher of mine once said, "If you can do anything else but act, save your time and money and do that!" He just pissed me off. I knew what I wanted. I wanted to act, goddammit! I wanted to get paid for my art, find recognition for my craft, and make a good living! I wanted to act more than I wanted the cozy cottage in Youngstown!

It boils down to sacrifice. What are you willing to give up to be an actor? For the first fifteen years of my career, I lived paycheck-to-paycheck, wore out my shoes, ate ramen noodles, and never took a vacation. I knew it was a sacrifice, but my desire to act was greater than my desire to visit Cancun. My parents and civilians (a civilian is everyone in the so-called real world who's not an actor) would often witness these breaks in my confidence and see the meager living I was struggling to make and gleefully tell me that I'd make a great high school principal. Or, had I thought about acting on TV? "I hear those guys on Friends make a lot of money! Or, what about becoming a car salesman?" This last bit of brilliance wrecked a perfectly fine relationship for me, as I didn't want to go out with a person who'd want to date a car salesman!!!

The civilians and most families may never understand. They really don't know what you're trying to do. There's a reason theatre kids sit at the same cafeteria table. They're a special, wonderful brew of crazy; passionate, curious, funny, and deeply lonely without a script in their hands. Your civilian friends will be disappointed and upset because you can't make their wedding in Greece as you're in a show or shooting a commercial. "Can't you just miss those three nights?" NO! You can't! Trust me, you'll write a lot of "I'm sorry" notes. My presence in the business today is a result of hard work, education, friendships, diligence, and adaptation. Let me be real. It's not an easy life. There are blows to your pride, sacrifices for sure, and rejections aplenty. However, in the final analysis, being an actor is a truly rich life full of growth, joy, fascinating artists, and the satisfaction of helping others make sense of their lives through the characters you create. Those civilians stuck in their cubes logging forms on the plumbing problems in unit D don't have this kind of calling. It's not a ministry to them. Through theatre, actors have the potential to alter the very course of society. By telling the truth, we shine the light on society's ills and often stir conversation that leads to a better life for us all. It's an awesome responsibility, and that's the only time I'm going to use the word "awesome" in this book!

There will be moments of true existential terror. This is the time to use your hands. When in doubt, take a minute to examine your dominant hand. Study it like you've never seen it before. Carefully make note of its lines and imperfections, and pay particular attention to its beauty. Now, think: "No one else in the world has my hand." You are truly enough. It says so right there on your hand.

Finally, you need to think about what success means for you. Write it down. Go back to it monthly and ask if what you've been doing is serving your goals. Realize, those goals may change over time—that is natural and legitimate. But hold yourself and what you do to both a purpose and a standard. Question: if your goal is the cover of *People Magazine* and you fail in that but are able to make enough to support yourself as a working actor, are you successful? If you can see progress, chances are you will stay in the game; if you are conscious of the challenge TO BE and you persevere, you've already had a measure of success. So, let's begin our journey. Avanti!

THE TOOLS OF THE ROOM

NOTE:
References

IN THIS BOOK, I'll be drawing on the following dramatic scripts to illustrate my teaching philosophy. Read the plays and watch *Boys Don't Cry*, an independent film.

Pipeline
Dominique Morisseau

The Piano Lesson
August Wilson

A Streetcar Named Desire
Tennessee Williams

Hamlet
William Shakespeare

Romeo and Juliet
William Shakespeare

Death of a Salesman
Arthur Miller

Boys Don't Cry
Kimberly Peirce

NOTE:
The Actor's Terror

We are all scared. We are all afraid of making fools of ourselves. We long for approval. It's natural. Actors want their work to land and find an audience. The health of your ego has a lot to do with whether you can handle the stresses of the profession. The actor's ego wants to be loved; it wants the extra curtain call and the audience lining up at the stage door to beg for autographs and selfies. Fortunate actors in a hit play can feed off this adoration. No wonder they get pissed when they don't get the best table or someone doesn't use oat milk in their latte! Adoration can turn a nice guy bad, and should never be confused with validation. We crave knowing that who we are and what we do is accepted, approved, and appreciated by others; it makes our striving worthwhile. Adoration is just a symptom of validation, not a goal. But even in this there is a pitfall.

In starting your journey towards being a working actor, you inevitably will encounter the guru acting teacher who carries himself like an oracle and convinces you he must have the final word. Does he not look the part? Does he not exude presence, authority, and an insider's knowledge? He's been around. He smokes unfiltered cigarettes. The environment this so-called acting guru creates is rich with fear. His disciples all long for a kind word from the fraud in the scarf and grey goatee. "Will he like my acting? Am I good enough?" As a sophomore at Emerson College, I was assigned an adviser—and yes, he had a scarf and grey beard. He took one look at the performance of my monologue and announced that I would only play nervous characters the rest of my life. I had nowhere to go with this career sentence. I was impressionable, but I was also tough and as I walked out of The Brimmer Street Theatre, I swore that I'd prove him wrong.

We come by our fear of disapproval and ridicule honestly. A young actor must trust their gut when shopping for a teacher, but they also need to ask questions. Is she a working actor? Does she have a proven track record in guiding young hearts and minds? Or is she a jerk that just wants adulation from her acolytes? What do her students say? Audit her acting class. If she doesn't let you do that, move on. If she does, are you willing to share your soul with her? An acting class is a very intimate world; trust, safety, and care are the hallmarks of a great classroom. This also applies to rehearsal rooms. Think strategically and critically.

As an actor, it's your job to ask questions at every level of your craft. However, the American educational system and its matrix for success is skewed towards teaching to the test. It requires that you regurgitate facts, not question their derivation, relevance, or importance. Test scores can surpass critical thinking in importance because they can lead to that elusive Ivy League spot or graduate school program.

This can be a stew of crazy for acting students because acting requires large portions of uncertainty, risk, and failure. However, it also prepares a young actor for a career of life-long learning. Artists traffic in questions, not answers; in process, not results. Thus, the actor's "test" requires patience, vulnerability, and true artistic courage. The amateur wants an answer, any answer. Just let it be done. The artist carries on through the mess of it all to find a truly original performance. And yes, it's a mess.

Jill Heinerth is the first female deep-sea cave diver. A true pioneer. She survived years of blatant sexism to become one of the foremost leaders in her art. She has explored worlds that no one on earth has seen, and lost over a hundred friends to diving deaths. One of her stories speaks to the actor's journey. Often, she will explore a cave that no human being has seen. She never knows what she'll find or what conditions lie before her. In her book, *Into the Planet*, Heinerth tells of one cave that nearly took her life. This particular cave was extremely delicate and as her feet touched the sand, silt began to fill the water; she lost her sense of direction as the silt covered her mask, rendering her blind. She had no idea which way was up or out. She had to live in that confusion and work her way out. She never quit. She lived in doubt for nearly an hour, knowing that silt was the cost of doing business. It comes with the territory. Actors explore the same kind of cave every day. It's called rehearsal!

Yes, I've had therapists and studied self-help books that tell me that fear is irrational. But have any one of these experts confronted the black terror of an opening night when you've only run the play once, and that was at four in the morning? Or found themselves on the set of a feature film with scores of technicians rolling their eyes, wondering if you'll ever get the scene done before the sun goes down? I maintain that if they had, they'd never say "it's just a play" or "it's only a silly film. Why worry?"

Consider the acting process as it relates to our sense of self and our need for approval and spiritual fulfillment. What sane human being would willingly walk into a cold, badly lit room and bare their soul to a table full of strangers, or stand in front of hundreds of tired audience members that are only in their seats for the chase scene? Again, I maintain, we come by our fear honestly.

How then to move forward when fear seems an unshakable obstacle to the acting process? Fear and relaxation are sworn enemies. If you're not working from a center of relief, the very act of performing will be a miserable chore and will curtail your career before it has a chance to blossom into a thriving livelihood. Let me just say that I am in some ways an expert in this matter. It's why I am sitting on my couch writing this book this morning. For thirty years I acted professionally without experiencing real terror, nerves, or stage fright. On the contrary, I was raring to go. While my cast mates were pacing in the wings, I was the guy telling jokes, cutting up with my dresser. Then in 2009, I played Michael, the narrator in Brian Friel's masterpiece, *Dancing at Lughnasa,* at The Florida Repertory Theatre. The recession of 2008 had come very close to shutting down The Rep. All of us were keenly aware that if this show sank, we might very well be the last act for The Rep and on the streets looking for jobs. In addition, our very nice and talented director had given only a few notes to me during the rehearsal—hardly any at all. I was essentially on my own. That, combined with the reality that I had literally pages of narration, left me feeling unhinged. It was the first preview. The stage manager called "places." I took up my position in the wings. And then it happened. I could feel my legs weakening. My heart raced, my upper lip broke out in beads of flop sweat, and my breathing (the source of relaxation) quickened and shortened. I knew that I had pages of words before me and the job of setting the mood for this wonderful play on my now sweaty back. I was in hell. It was all I could do to find my mark in the dark once the stage went black. As the lights came up, and I started to speak, I became fully self-conscious about every line I spoke as if I were in Acting I again at Emerson College. But I made it. I survived. The show got a rave in *The Wall Street Journal* and the production saved the theatre. We were the talk of the town. All was well. But I was in trouble. I felt something had broken in my resolve and I spent every day in terror of "places." I continued to act for several more years with stage fright as my constant companion. What used to be the joy of my life had become torture. In 2014, I quit. I have not looked back. I miss the camaraderie, the laughter, and the intimacy. However, I get all of that today from being the director or teacher in the room, and from writing this book for you. Sometimes your fear pushes you towards a place where your potential feels greater, as it did with me. But when it doesn't, you have to recognize and deal with it if you are ever going to feel joy from acting.

SO, WHAT TO DO?

Place your attention on something other than yourself. If your focus is on you, then your fear will be great. If your dreaded self-conscious tells you "It's all about you," you have created an unnecessary whirlwind of silt for yourself. To get yourself out of this mess and reduce stress, focus on the moment at hand and how you can change the other person. This will reduce the stress. When you are afraid, you activate your flight or fight response, and you stop breathing normally. As an actor, you need to build your breathing technique and learn to drop your breath to the center of your body so that instead of tensing up, you are living in a world where the dominant mode of communication is relief. To help get you there, I highly recommend yoga, meditation, prayer, beta blockers, therapy, or all of the above. However, I implore you to study the work of Kristin Linklater. In my experience, her work gets to the heart of integrated body breath and voice work that supports and fuels your creativity and subjugates self-conscious fear. Free breath leads to the relaxation of the body and invigoration of the mind. The very best teacher of the Linklater progression is Louis Colaianni. Louis's work is transformative. He creates a magic room and transports the actor to a genuine openness that reaches the depth of their soul and unleashes true, vibrant, creative intimacy. Louis's approach to this work and what it accomplishes has inspired me every day for fifteen years. From Louis, I learned that at the root of my fake "actor voice" was my fear that my true voice couldn't possibly be interesting enough. He reminded me that an audience doesn't want to hear your voice, they want to hear you. Finally, through Louis I understood that the connection of heart to heart, breath to breath, thought to thought, impulse to impulse, is what makes acting dangerous and satisfying; that we must risk rejection to be authentic—a small price to pay for seeking the truth.

To combat stage fright and nerves, you should also focus your energy on building a strong foundation of technique. Technique simply means the ability to perform well when all systems are not working. It's an "A-". Most professionals only employ it when things are not working (like going on stage with a 104-degree fever, dancing on a broken toe, or playing a comedy for screaming drunks). Once you find your way as an actor, you rely less on technique and focus more on pure creation, knowing that the leg work (technique) has already been done. Once, Morgan Freeman was asked what he did to prepare for a role. He said, "I read the script." I had to laugh, but at his age and experience, he is a master and only needs the story. Freeman hasn't thought about technique for decades.

This book is a guide for you to begin building a working

technique for yourself. Someday you can call yourself a master, but to be a true master, you need, as Malcolm Gladwell put it, ten thousand hours invested in your craft.

Let's work on that first hour together.

NOTE:
Engagement: Are you listening to me?

This may be the single most important note, and it's the one technique which we can practice (or ignore) in our daily lives. We receive sound waves with the ears, but we receive literal meaning, tone of voice, volume, subtext, implication, and body language with our minds and hearts.

How many times have you heard someone say, "I told you that ten minutes ago?" What was actually going on that made you so dull as not to remember that your brother needed the car at 5 p.m.? Your ears are perfectly healthy and yet, you clearly did not listen to him. Something much more important kept you from listening fully. You may not have looked at your brother when he told you he needed the car at 5 p.m. Maybe you were preoccupied with a video game. You may have just tuned him out. It's a bad habit that will not serve you well in other interpersonal relationships, like work, romance, or school.

How do you engage and tune in to the people and things around you? Awareness. It is vital to decode what is coming to you so that you can process, retain, and react to information. You have to see, hear, and feel what is around you to understand and assess the messages being sent your way. You don't get a memo… you have to do it. What is around you right now? What is it telling you? How does that make you feel? What are you going to do about it?

To actively engage in your surroundings and the people within it, you can use another tool in your human arsenal. Empathy. Empathy lets you see beyond yourself and your own needs and makes it easier to read delicate situations. Empathy begins with awareness and can be strengthened. Start by making eye contact! Imagine how you would feel if someone saw you as you really are, and not as that person expected you to be? By really seeing you, that person is creating a safe space in which you can express your vulnerabilities. They allow you to breathe and release your fears and hopes without judgment.

When we practice empathy in our daily lives, we learn to build another helpful quality: intimacy. Intimacy grows from empathy and is the key to exciting acting. Intimacy is vulnerable and messy; it is a soul exposed, naked, and truthful. We've all been to a play and thought, 'These people are not connected.' That's because there was no intimacy. It's not easy. Sharing ourselves and accepting another's messy truth is a risk and, rightly, should scare us. Not knowing how people will react to your authentic self can be terrifying—whether it's you as a person or as the character in a play.

Furthermore, what happens when you're called to play an emotionally fraught scene while never having actually listened to anyone in your life? Good news! You can learn. A new habit of connection can be built by practicing intimate listening in your personal life and by taking and mastering a good Fundamentals of Acting class.

Trust me, this listening business is a lifelong practice. But take care, as this note comes with a warning. You will encounter people with whom you cannot manage intimacy. You must read the room and protect yourself. Intimacy needs safety. It's not for every scenario. However, it must be part of your technique for rehearsal and performance.

Your ability to empathize with another is crucial, particularly on-camera. Watch any film or TV show and observe how much of the picture is people just listening. I urge you to observe your listening habits this week. Just notice them and slowly, with a safe person (they need not even know), practice empathy and intimate listening. I'm not a betting man, but I lay odds that you will be a richer actor for this work. Do you hear me?

NOTE:
What's the story?

For my money, great acting is based on good, old-fashioned storytelling. And storytelling breaks down this way:

Once upon a time…

After studying the text for character clues, (what you say about yourself and what others say about you) and unearthing the message of the play, determine what you want your story to be. Write your own. Be specific. Base it in the text. Determine what the playwright is trying to say with her play and figure out where your character fits in that story. Decide what your role is. What is your character's purpose in the play? Think in terms of story not just character. And then ask what do I want to say about my Hamlet? Am I a kid who grows up or a rebel looking for a cause? You'll find that once you know what you are trying to say (your point of view, your opinion) the easier the execution. Understanding your character's function in the play gives your performance structure.

It's necessary to determine what your character needs. Think of your own personal drama. What do you want? A career in theatre? To be a movie star? A home in the country? Four blond-haired kids? Now ask yourself how MUCH do you need these things and what will happen to you if you're not featured on the cover of *People*? What will become of you if you can't have children?

Here are some examples. Notice, I use the word need, not want. There is a clear distinction. Want is casual. We can survive without that extra scoop of ice cream. Need is life and death. We may live our whole lives only consciously thinking of what we want and never looking at what we need.

So, what does your character need? Here are some examples:

Hamlet NEEDS to **revenge his father's murder.**

Blanche in *A Streetcar Named Desire* NEEDS **a sanctuary.**

Juliet in *Romeo and Juliet* NEEDS **to love whom she desires.**

Nya in *Pipeline* NEEDS **to save her son's life.**
Brandon in the film *Boys Don't Cry* NEEDS **to be accepted by others.**

Boy Willie in *The Piano Lesson* NEEDS **to sell the family piano to become a man.**

NOTE:
Given Circumstances

The given circumstances of the play are rich with possibilities for the actor. Make note of them as they are the base of most of your acting choices. The given circumstances include:

WHERE ARE YOU?
At a park, in a church, a cemetery? How does that space make you feel?

WHAT TIME IS IT?
Decade, century, season, hour? How does the time impact the scene?

WHO ARE YOU WITH?
Your family, a strange man on the bus? Your child? Be specific about the feelings each of these relationships bring out in you.

WHAT HAPPENED THE MOMENT BEFORE THE SCENE STARTED?
What emotional, physical space are you in as the scene commences?

NOTE:
So Now What?

Ask yourself which is more important: what you do onstage or what you say? In any genre of theatre, it's what happens between the lines that is critical for the actor to understand; that's psychological. Whether you focus on what the character says or what he does, you must answer the question "why?" Furthermore, the greatest American director, Elia Kazan, put it this way. He said that his job as a director was to help the actor turn psychology into behavior. So you must ask of your character, what physical actions do they take to achieve their goals?

Hamlet hides away from friends and family *to muster his resolve.*

Blanche dims all the harsh light in the seedy apartment *to make her surroundings more palatable.*

Juliet plots to run away from home *to be with Romeo.*

Nya nearly kills herself *trying to keep her son from dying.*

Brandon hides his identity *to be accepted.*

Boy Willie conspires *to steal the piano from his sister Berniece.*

What do they DO? Then ask; HOW do they do it? Blanche pours a glass of whiskey very differently from Hamlet. You walk into a classroom very differently from your friend Jessy.

Once you know what the character needs, ask what does he DO to get it? What actions does he take? What is he willing to do to get what he needs and what tactics does he use to win?

Hamlet *employs a group of actors to re-enact his father's murder.*

Blanche *drinks to dull the horror of her surroundings and seduces men to feel wanted.*

Juliet *enlists her maid's help so that she can run away with Romeo.*

Nya *confronts her son, his school, her ex, and herself.*

Brandon *wraps his body in bandages and dresses as a man to find acceptance in the straight world of Nebraska.*

Boy Willie *persuades his friend Lymon to steal the piano for him.*

NOTE:
What's Stopping You?

Characters need to overcome obstacles. Without them, there is no conflict. No conflict means no fun. The audience delights in the struggle. So, ask yourself: what are the OBSTACLES standing in the way that keep her from getting what she needs?

Hamlet needs *to expose the usurper king and avenge his father's murder*. His obstacles include his *lack of courage and confidence that he will be believed*, *his mother's love for his assassin uncle*, *a court content with the status quo* and *his feelings for Ophelia*.

Blanche wants *to be safe and adored* as a beautiful gardenia, but time is against her—the edges of the gardenia are turning brown. She wants *poetry and moonlight in a world loudly hawking plastic flowers to the dead* under stark streetlamps while gentleman suitors become sweaty, lust-filled animals.

Juliet is *stymied by the control of her parents and family loyalty*.

Nya needs *to keep her son safe*. Her obstacles are *the racist world, Omari's school, Omari's rage, and her ex's obtuseness*.

Brandon's obstacle is *the homophobic world of Nebraska in 1990*.

Boy Willie's family and Sutter's Ghost all *fight to keep the piano safe* in Berniece's parlor.

We don't go to the movies to watch a victim sit and weep.

We want a fighter. <u>Characters need to take-action</u>; to reach, to change, to radicalize their world, even if that action is simple. My dear friend Craig Bockhorn, an extraordinary actor, was an understudy for Anton Chekhov's *The Seagull* produced in Central Park by The New York Shakespeare Festival with a star-studded cast featuring Meryl Streep. He told me this story that says it all. Mike Nichols, a brilliant artist, was at the helm and asked Ms. Streep what she wanted to do in a scene and she replied simply, "Mike, I just want to have a cup of tea and forget about my problems." Nichols said, "Brilliant! And my job is to make that absolutely impossible for that to happen!" In this way, everything that happens to Arkadina is an obstacle for her. She has to fight throughout. We can be passive in life but keep your need for peace and rainbows off the stage. Give me a good struggle any day.

NOTE:
How badly do you need it?

Essentially, what are the STAKES (what's the bet)? How much are you willing to gamble to win your hand of poker? I often call it "your skin in the game." If you find yourself describing your need and stakes as "I kinda wanna" or "Well it's a little like...", I maintain you have not done your homework. All of us have a driving motivation in our lives. Find your character's.

I need to be respected in both the academic and professional theatrical worlds and that is why I worked so hard in my career and carefully wrote this book. And, when I tell you that things could go very wrong if I don't keep working hard and don't write a great book. I'm telling you the truth. The stakes in my life are very high. My work must lead to success because it's more than just my passion; it's my livelihood. So, break it down. What does your character NEED? What will happen if she doesn't get what she needs? STAKES. When a director says she doesn't know what you're playing, nine times out of ten, it's because you haven't worked these elements out in a way that you can act on them.

Hamlet's NEED is to *avenge his father's death*. The STAKES are that if he fails, he will *destroy his father's legacy*.

Blanche NEEDS to *find sanctuary*. The STAKES are that if she doesn't, she will wither away in obscurity.

Juliet NEEDS to *follow her heart*. The STAKES are if she fails, *she will pass from the control of her father to the control of Paris*, a dreadful man her father has chosen, and spend her life chained to a cipher.

Nya NEEDS to *keep her son safe*. If she fails, she will disintegrate and he will surely end up dead.

Brandon NEEDS to *live fully in his skin*. The STAKES are that if he doesn't, he has to return to the violent, hateful, homophobic world he has desperately tried to leave behind.

Boy Willie NEEDS *the money* from the sale of the piano. The STAKES are that if he can't make that happen, he'll end up a poor sharecropper with no power.

NOTE:
"So That"—Go Deeper

Sometimes it's necessary to think as a playwright. Consider not just what you NEED (objective) and what you DO to achieve it (actions) but also how winning your objective will improve your life (or just a single moment in your life).

To find that, add the power of SO THAT to your preparation. I need to win this argument SO THAT I can run the race and receive the applause I so desperately seek from the crowd.

In *The Handmaid's Tale*, the sublime Elizabeth Moss's character, Offred, is repeatedly assaulted. Attending *The Hollywood Reporter Roundtable*, Moss was asked how she handled that acting challenge. She said that she chose to have Offred check out, disassociate. Her need as the character is to survive so she checks out, disassociates, while the assault is happening. Offred has to go away SO THAT she can live another day. To live another day is always a good goal!

Here are more examples:

I want him to give me the gun
SO THAT **I can stop freaking out.**

I want to make her laugh
SO THAT **she'll remember how much
she once loved me.**

I want to flatter him
SO THAT **he never doubts my power.**

I want to teach her about my pain
SO THAT **she'll forgive my anger.**

I want to convince him of the rightness of my plan
SO THAT **my plan is the one we use to break out of prison.**

NOTE:
Relationships

You have hundreds of relationships in your life: your mom, your dad, best friend, favorite teacher, beloved grandmother, secret crush. Each of these people makes you feel a particular way and each brings out specific behavior in you. Specifying the relationships you have in a scene and how they make your character feel will lead to dynamic physical, vocal, and emotional choices. But you must be brutally honest; your mom may make you feel free and confident but your older sister (though you love her) may make you feel unattractive. We have friends who make us flirt and friends who make us want to hide under a rock. We have relationships that lead us to danger and relationships that fill us with shame. And because drama is change, you can track your performance by how your relationships transition through the arc of the play. Relationships are fundamental to provocative behavior. Understanding the acting power of relationships will also offer vocal and physical variety. Your tone of voice and verbal energy reflects your relationship to the receiver. Your voice takes on a very different color when you're talking to your girlfriend as compared to speaking with your parents. We speak faster to friends our age and much slower to our great-grandparents.

NOTE:
Changes

Ask yourself, are you willing to allow yourself to be changed by your partner? And do you have the emotional need necessary to change your partner? Ask yourself how much am I willing to let into my heart? When you're in this state, you will have access to your vulnerability. And a vulnerable actor is someone an audience must closely watch. Vulnerability leads to mystery and suspense. Vulnerability keeps all of us, fellow actors and audience, rapt. Breathe in your partners and release yourself on your breath into them.

NOTE:
Question Your Heart

The New York Times ran an editorial from the billionaire investor Warren Buffett. In it, Buffett advised that reacting with passion and honesty, on impulse, is a dangerous technique; more-over, it is a sign of weakness that leads to financial ruin. Buffett and other revered civilians are obsessed with this idea of not reacting to other people's energy. And this is supposed to help mankind evolve? I was enraged. The willingness to allow someone's energy, spirit, thoughts, to change you and the desire to change them in kind is the essence of talking and listening, of staying present with another human. This energy is the base of all great acting. Actors are reactionary. Temperamental. It's our gift and our responsibility.

As a business model of behavior becomes increasingly more revered, people become less accustomed to recognizing basic human instincts and impulses. So, it's necessary to stop and ask yourself, "what's really going on with me?" This takes rehabilitating our feeling systems. You certainly know what is acceptable in polite company: the socialized response. But what of your gut reactions? In fact, if you observe your responses moment to moment, you may see that you've gone days without responding honestly to your friends, family, and co-workers. There is nothing wrong with being polite, but if you live a life actively avoiding your truth, how are you to discover what your character is feeling in their heart of hearts and moment by moment? Recognizing and ACCEPTING your heart is a practice as much as yoga, tennis, or your religion. Your acting demands it. However, society conditions us to believe that the impulsive display of emotion is dangerous. It also tells us that there are positive emotions (like joy) and negative ones (like anger). But anger is only dangerous if you act dangerously.

NOTE:

Drama Is Not About Success

From our earliest years, we are encouraged to behave in a way that subjugates emotional responses. In kindergarten we are told "use your words"; at home we got "stair time" if we yelled or carried on. But sit on your reactions long enough, and you'll lose all sense of yourself. Speak your anger, tell your truth, or be consumed by repression. However, be patient. It took nineteen years to build this habit, it may take a little while to alter it. Let civilians sit on their feelings. If money, at the expense of passion and truth, is what you want, I say, "Godspeed." Just leave me out of it. Time is too short to lie all day long.

Drama is about the struggle to make sense of our lives. All art is an attempt to answer the question, "Why are we here?" So, look for the opportunities to fail, to be overcome. It will give your characters richness. We in the dark will root for you to win! We go to the movies to watch others lead our lives for us. From the comfort of our seats, we learn about our own lives by watching others strive where we're too timid to even make an attempt.

NOTE:
Be a Character Sleuth

Your homework begins by asking questions about your character:

- How do they identify?
- What pronouns?
- Money?
- Age?
- Religion?
- Spirituality?
- Dark secrets?
- Private passions?
- Thinker?
- Feeler?
- Traumas?
- Shames?

- Political affiliation?
- Racist?
- Optimist?
- Pessimist?
- Sexual history?
- Education?
- Mental health?
- Physical health?
- Medications?
- Fantasies?
- Loves?
- If the house was on fire, what would they rush in to save?

NOTE:

Consider Your Label: "Who Are You?"

Whether we know it or not, we self-label. Some may be labels we have been branded with by our parents, teachers, or peers. Others may be labels we take on to protect our true selves, presenting a different image to the world to attract or distract attention. But identities can be fragile and labels can alter under adverse circumstances. We lose some self-awareness and struggle with tension when forced to confront a new label or maintain a false one.

Interestingly, you can use this idea when building the arc of a character. For example, how does Hamlet label himself in Act I? Now, how does that label change scene by scene? Perhaps Act I equals "failure"; Act V might be "a worthy son".

NOTE:
"What's the Dance?"

How do you sit, stand, cross the stage? Are you:
- A sloth?
- A soldier?
- A dancer?
- Uptight?
- Relaxed?

Do you walk on the earth, above the earth, or in the earth? Where is your center of gravity? Are you cerebral or physical? Are you in touch with your soul or shut down? What chakra are you leading with? Do you think more than you feel? Do you walk in straight lines or serpentine curves? Do you make eye contact or hide?

For the story to be clear and dramatic (remember that drama is change) you must change your character's movement pattern and over-all physicality from the beginning to the end of the story. This holds true even if you only have a three-page scene.

HAMLET begins the night *the shell of a man, slouched and mopey;* he finishes the play *an elegant, heroic leader — a true prince.*

In *A Streetcar Named Desire,* BLANCHE comes onstage as *a grand lady of the South;* she leaves for the insane asylum *suffering from acute PTSD.*

In *Romeo and Juliet*, we meet JULIET as a *flitty, flirtatious youngster* who is transformed into *a woman of passion and resolve.*

In *Pipeline*, NYA begins her journey *unsound and lost.* By the play's end, she is *securely standing straight and tall.*

In *Boys Don't Cry*, we first see BRANDON *nervously attempting to create his true self.* By the movie's end, he *has realized his true self—body and spirit.*

In *The Piano Lesson*, BOY WILLIE moves like *a haunted man.* By the play's end, *all his troubles have left his body.*

It's necessary to extrovert your choices physically so that if we were to watch the play without sound we'd know what was going on. I remember seeing Ingmar Bergman's Hamlet at The Brooklyn Academy of Music performed in Swedish. I didn't (and still don't) speak a word of Swedish but I knew exactly what was going on. So, take a dance class; study mime; take a mask class with my brilliant friend, Carine Montbertrand! Study Chaplin and Keaton and Lucille Ball and Melissa McCarthy.

NOTE:
Look to Nature: Animal Studies

The natural world teems with visceral behaviors that can inspire your imagination. What physical traits can you bring to your role from an animal study?

- Suffering from anxiety? *Work on a squirrel.*
- An old patriarch? *Study a silverback ape.*
- A sexy movie star? *Become a leopard.*
- A comic character with a strange voice? *Imagine a hyperventilating frog.*
- A terrifying judge? *Screech like an eagle devouring its prey.*

NOTE:

The Chicken or the Egg?

Are you scared because you're running? Or running because you're scared? Consider this scenario: You're walking down a dark, deserted street late at night looking for your car when suddenly you hear something behind you. You jump and take a fight position, or you run away. Fight or flight, yes? It doesn't matter that it was just a stray dog wrestling a bone from the trash, your reaction is legit. But consider. What was the feeling you had? Surely, your breath changed, your nervous system went into overdrive, and your mouth dried. All of these reactions are the same whether we are terrified, enraged, in love, or overjoyed. Now add the given circumstances of the play and your character's response to the particular stress of the moment (remember stress reveals character) and you have yourself the beginning of a fine performance. Furthermore, as it is based in a physical reality (in this case running in the dark and clenching your fists), you can reliably repeat that to bring yourself to the emotional needs of the moment. It's not hocus-pocus, it's training—using your imagination, breath, and body to work together to create a credible physical reaction that reveals and establishes your character.

Consider these other physical/emotional reactions: lurching through the front door and collapsing in a chair; running wildly up a flight of steps; standing nonchalantly underneath a lamppost; cowering in the fetal position; hiding under the covers, walking with a crutch, gesturing with your non-dominant hand. Remember, your body doesn't know it's not make-believe!

NOTE:
Artistic Opinion—Play Your Violin

I was discussing the similarities in creating theatrical art and music with Queno, a talented Julliard trained musician. I think he captured a fundamental aspect of both. I said that so many young actors don't have a clear point of view that illuminates the material and puts their personal touch on the role. Think of it: Meryl Streep's Lady Macbeth will be very different from Nicole Kidman's. Each of these genius actors have vastly different backgrounds, unique opinions and approaches to Shakespeare's classic. Queno likened it to rosin on a violin bow. If there is no rosin, the strings make no music, no sound at all. They have no opinion. When building a character, I think of emotional Velcro. What sticks? All that you do in your life: romances, politics, spirituality, education, disappointments, failures, fantasies and dreams, builds your artistic opinions and informs your approach to your work and your character. Your opinions are your rosin.

NOTE:
Validation and Rejection

I believe that our greatest desire is for validation. Wouldn't it be nice, if every morning our best, most trusted friend, would hold our hands, look us in the eye and very gently tell us that we are great, that we're doing the right thing, that it will all pay off, and we'll find love soon!

Likewise, our greatest fear is rejection. It's what keeps most of us from reacting honestly and authentically in our lives. We lack the courage to do so because we are afraid of being rejected, afraid of being publicly humiliated. We learn this lesson on the playground as children. We try to blend in and hang with the cool kids, the right gang, so we won't be identified with the losers and freaks. (The same kids who sign up for drama class!) *West Side Story* had it dead on. So, when building a scene, you can always add these two elements to your character's needs. They will never fail you: Seek validation; avoid rejection.

NOTE:
It's Not About You

Pity the poor actor who wants to make the role all about themselves. The wrong-headed acting teacher (grey goatee) who instills this technique only hurts the actor.

You are not Hamlet. Hamlet only exists in Shakespeare's mind. However, the text obligates you to accomplish certain dramatic choices to effectively tell the story so that the audience sees

Hamlet through you and gets their money's worth. The approach that says play Hamlet as if Hamlet were you; that he reacts as you would react, fails to respect the text and our emotional limitations. An imagination is a wonderful tool. Dream a little. Make-believe is vital.

NOTE:
Discoveries

Drama is change. Change demands discoveries. Identify where exactly your character changes in the play. Frame those moments. Theatricalize, extrovert those moments so that you're painting a canvas for the audience to witness your journey. Think back to when Romeo discovers that Juliet is a Capulet and his sworn enemy. Or when Hamlet's father comes from the grave to tell him that he was murdered by Hamlet's uncle. Consider the moment Biff, in *Death of a Salesman*, discovers that his beloved father is cheating on his mom with a hooker. The beauty of discoveries is that the new information, awareness, understanding will knock your character off his feet. Creatively speaking, it's always delicious to experience and explore that character's moment of discovery because the next moment is so rich with possibilities. That space between actions is often the most instructive. Jazz artists know this. Improv in jazz often leads to surprising discovery. The quartet gets lost in the Improv, and the journey back to the melody is where the fun lies for the artist.

Screenwriters understand that all great scripts begin at (A) and end with a final shot (Z). It's old school and kind of corny but there is an old screenwriting trick: Sad/Glad/Mad/Scared. If your lead character starts the scene sad, by the end of the scene they must have changed into one of the other 3: Glad, Mad or Scared! Clearly, it's never quite that cut and dried, but it does make the actor think: what do I discover, and how do I change in this scene?

NOTE:

Think Faster

We all think and act faster under enormous stress. And all characters in any decent play are under terrific stress. So "think faster". Act ON the lines, which means forget all manners and act on the stimulus (often found in the middle of another character's lines or physicality). Waiting for the other characters to finish their thoughts leads to ponderous, banal performances. Thinking faster builds pace and adds to the forward momentum of a well-written piece. Modern audiences are accustomed to picking up the story quickly. Even kindergartners can tell you what the story is about after just a few minutes. When your director tells you the pace is too slow, think faster, react faster. Need it more!

NOTE:

Acting on Impulse

Our primary responses get us in trouble, especially as we age and those responses become socially unacceptable. It's one thing to kick your chair and scream for another chicken nugget at age three; it's quite another to do so at age thirteen—not only will your impulse to scream for food not be rewarded, you may never be given another chicken nugget again in your life!

As an actor, build awareness of your primary impulses—your immediate, uncensored responses to stimuli and situations. These are your lifeblood. Recognizing them will help you find them in your character and create a more authentic and visceral depiction.

Think back to what it was like in second grade when you had the answer to the math problem and your hand shot up faster than you could think it. You didn't stop to wonder about being polite or even correct, you were simply in the moment. You responded immediately without thinking because that response was ingrained in you, part and parcel of your character, focus, and energy. Understanding your character's impulses and responding to them in the moment is challenging—especially because in civilian life, we are conditioned to think before speaking or acting and then do so in socially appropriate words and ways (think back to the chicken nugget). Our upbringing often distances us from being keenly in touch with our shifting impulses. But that ability is imperative in acting—immediacy of action (or impulse) is what makes a character exciting to watch; it viscerally connects us to what the character is experiencing—no thought, just reaction.

I often quote Thorton Wilder's classic, *Our Town*. At the end of Act III, Emily asks the Stage Manager, "Do any human beings ever realize life while they live it—every, every minute?" The Stage Manager answers, "Humans indeed do not realize life, except for perhaps the saints and poets, maybe." I put actors in this category as well. We must live every moment fully so we can develop the temperament for the art form. We must be able to laugh easily, cry quickly, and feel the world's pain instantly. Trust your gut, it will never fail you.

NOTE:
Is it Beer or Champagne?

Genre, (or the style of the writing), determines many of your acting choices. Chekhov is not Shakespeare; *Hamilton* is not *Mean Girls*; oil is not watercolors; silk is not wool; Bach is not Beethoven; curry is not ketchup; sitcoms are not action movies. Go further, ask: what's the time signature? Is it a waltz or a rhumba? Read as much as you can; watch as much as you can. Build your awareness of what the various genres are and study the choices actors make to successfully play them.

NOTE:
Where Did That Come From?

Have you ever been called out on a lie you told? Remember that feeling of defensiveness that overcame you? You were reacting out of guilt. Or consider your first secret crush as a teenager. Remember the blush that blazed across your sweaty face at the lunch table when Patty Englehart asked if she could join you in a light repast of meatloaf, tater tots, and whole milk? You were reacting out of love (or perhaps lust)! What's on your character's mind? What is his greatest fear, wildest secret?

NOTE:

Make Sense Of It

The five senses are: taste, touch, hearing, sight, and smell. What do you hear? Does the caw of a raven excite or terrify you? How about the coo of a dove? Consider the loud knocking on the door in the murder scene in *Macbeth*. The knock is terrifying. What do you see? An artist sees the color and composition in the room. An actor sees the inherent drama in the room. The insurance agent sees the risk in the room. A shark sees everything as dinner! What do you feel? Does silk make you passionate; does the calloused hand of your husband stir safety in your heart? What feelings do your senses create in you? For more on this, consider reading Lee Strasberg's great book on method acting, *A Dream of Passion: The Development of the Method*. It's brilliant!

NOTE:

Words, Words, Words

Actors trained for the theatre make the most of text. The text is the actual dialogue, not to be confused with behavior. Study any of Meryl Streep's roles and watch how she handles the text. Text analysis is vital in all acting but mandatory in playing the classics like Shakespeare, where the actor must also help the audience understand words and syntax foreign to the modern ear. Good text work is similarly fundamental to voice-overs, commercials, and books-on-tape. It's abundantly clear that when an actor has not made a text choice, they don't know what their character wants.

When an actor has not based her characterization on the text, her performance is untethered and unclear. When an actor doesn't support her characterization by how she attacks text, the performance will also lack clarity. When this happens, I submit the actor really doesn't understand what her character wants (her objective), so then neither do we.

What is making a text choice? Read the play. What is the most important word or phrase in each thought? Underline it. Say it out loud. Now, change it to another word or phrase in each thought in the sentence. Say it out loud. Hear the difference. Changing the stress in a single word or thought changes meaning and intention.

Here is a horrible line of text:

"I told them to come on Monday."

Now, listen to what happens when you change the stress:

I **TOLD** them to come on Monday.
(*Did you write them?*)

I told them to come on **MONDAY.**
(Not on Tuesday.)

I told **THEM** to come on Monday.
(Not the other kids.)

Now, here is a great line of text. Consider the change in meaning with each of these different stresses:

To **BE** or not to be, that is the question.

To be or **NOT** to be, that is the question.

To be or not to be, **THAT** is the question.

To be or not to be, that is the **QUESTION**.

A few helpful rules to act by:

1. Do NOT stress pronouns unless you are making a comparison:

    YOU did this. **HE** did that.
    HE went home; **I** came here.

2. When in doubt, stress the *most interesting words*.

3. Do not stress "to be" verbs. These are:
    be | am | is | are | was | were | been

4. Stress *active verbs* first and *nouns* second.

NOTE:
Shakespeare: Speak the Speech

Make all your characters great speakers and great teachers. Just do it. And make them really smart with twice your vocabulary! Elizabethans had larger vocabularies than we do and were well-trained to support their arguments with the spoken word.

Stress antithesis (opposites such as black/white, cold/hot), whenever possible. It will help clarify your argument.

It is vital to stress the final image in the verse as that is where the crux of your intention is held. The final image is either the end of a thought or the springboard to a clarifying or new thought that begins with the next line.

Set speeches break down into three parts: the thesis, the supporting materials, the conclusion. This is not an accident. Your character knows that the listener learns best from this construction (think term paper in high school). This kind of construction helps your character teach the other characters and believe that they've achieved their goal.

Identify plot points. It's the actor's job to stress those. Your director will love you for this skill.

Identify the imagery in the text. Is it dark or light? Romantic? Pessimistic? What does that tell you about your character's state of being?

What are the sensory elements at work? Experience them as you say them. Elizabethans were much more in touch with their senses than we are and used them to illustrate their feelings.

Learn sonnets. It will keep you sharp.

Strive for eloquence. It is just as dangerous to swamp a text with too much feeling as it is to be just a storyteller. The ability to express yourself through heightened speech in moments of great emotion is the hallmark of great acting.

NOTE:
The Almighty Laugh

The brilliant Martin LaPlatney told me a story about the difference between drama and comedy:

DRAMA: *A man is lost in the woods for six months. Starving, he stumbles, at last, onto a farm where his host feeds him a great banquet. He eats all the beef and cakes and drinks all the wine, burps, and smiles.*

COMEDY: *A man is lost in the woods for six months. Starving, he stumbles, at last, onto a farm where his host feeds him a great banquet. He eats all the beef and cakes and drinks all the wine, burps and smiles. Then he wipes his mouth with his napkin and proceeds to eat the plates!!*

You see, the happy man took it one step further into the ridiculous. Crazy, but based in reality. After all, had he not starved for six months? I guess he was still hungry!

For comedy to succeed, the character must be fully open, fully vulnerable to the powers that he is fighting against. The greater the pain, loss, and humiliation, the funnier. The actor must not stand in the way for fear of making a fool of himself; if so, he will not succeed in comedy. So, get over yourself!

One of the world's greatest playwrights, Samuel Beckett wrote: "Nothing funnier than pain." Tears and laughter. It's why we laugh when someone slips on a banana peel! It's also the premise of all of Woody Allen's films. Here are a few rules for comedy:

1. PLAY IT STRAIGHT.

You can't be funny. Trust the writing.

2. IDENTIFY THE JOKE.

What part do you play in it?

Don't try to get a laugh out of a set-up. At the beginning of a comedy, the audience needs to learn the rules of the game. Each play is a universe unto itself, so before the laughs roll, the audience needs to understand the premise of the evening's entertainment. Tell the story clearly, establish character and conflict, THEN get them rolling in the aisles. To understand this better, study the work of the tremendous writer Alan Ayckbourn—just splendid construction in every one of his plays. The great comics are patient.

3. DON'T MOVE ON A LAUGH LINE.

Release the tension for a split second after the joke/laugh then move onto a new focus and start all over again.

Risa Brainin is one of the finest directors in the American Theatre. I worked with her in *Noises Off* at Indiana Rep. I loved every minute of her rehearsal room which was a space of true creative exploration. One of her rehearsal tools was an improv she calls "Giggles and Weeps". The actor creates two stories. "Giggles" is the happiest moment in their character's life and "Weeps" is the saddest. The effect of the improv in rehearsing *Noises Off* was to take a brilliant farce and give it a sense of humanity. It wasn't just for the laughs we played. Thus, the stage was populated by fully three-dimensional creations. It's a lesson for all of us playing comedy. Create all aspects of your character.

4. USE CLEAN SPEECH WITH CRISP FINAL CONSONANTS.

5. DON'T ADD PAUSES.

Comedy tends to move fast. Look at all the actors in *The Marvelous Mrs. Maisel*. They ooze pace. Faster is funnier!

However, do hold for the laugh, breathe with the audience, let them have their fun, then crest the laugh, and say your next line or complete the stage business. Actors unaccustomed to playing a raucous comedy find themselves at a loss when an audience is convulsing with laughter for thirty, sometimes forty-five seconds at a clip. What to do when that happens? You don't want to step on the laugh (curtail it) but still, you're out there with nothing to do. When asked by the actor, Ron Silver, what to do when an audience is laughing long and hard, Mike Nichols, the famous director said, "But Ron, they're not there, don't worry." To which Silver said, "I don't get it." Nichols replied, "They're not there. People aren't there three times: when they're orgasming, when they sneeze, and when they convulse with laughter."

Trust me, holding for a huge laugh is like a shot of all the world's greatest drugs blended in one glorious smoothie. It is intoxicating and makes up for all those tedious hours in the room trying to crack the mystery of the laugh.

Most people in life don't know they are funny or think what they are doing will elicit a laugh from their co-workers or spouse. However, actors playing in comedies know that when done well, they will get plenty of laughs. Likewise, the character must not know that they are funny—unless playing a clown or a cutup. Think Steve Carell in *The Office* or Ricky Gervais in the British *The Office*.

For comic acting there is always a sense of how best to achieve the laugh. This is not just the actor's work but very much organized by the director. Actors need someone to watch and help them understand if what they are doing is reading as funny (the truth is, if an actor could see themselves, they wouldn't need a director)! "Funny" is often the result of countless hours in rehearsal exploration. It's screwy because the character must be completely innocent in the moment; fully unaware of an audience. However, the actor knows exactly what she is doing and to what end she must calibrate her performance to land the laugh.

Improvisation is a necessary building block for comic technique. It teaches the actor to truly listen and act on impulse. But it only goes so far in a comedy based on a play or screenplay. A director needs to set (freeze) the show so that it runs exactly to plan each performance or take. Improv is freer and not intended to be repeated. I worked with a brilliant improv actor. She was a wonder of invention. She had the room in stitches every day for the first half of the process but would never repeat her stage business or say her lines in approximately the same way. Though amazing, her improv technique could only go so far in the high-speed farce I was directing which required precise timing and consistency. The other actors needed her to settle into her choices in order to do their work. Therefore, I had to pick her best improvs and set those in stone so that we as a company could achieve a unified approach to the show. The trick is to give the appearance that what you are doing is being done for the very first time, not meticulously rehearsed for 142 hours.

NOTE:

Musical Theatre

Great musical actors are great actors. Period. Telling the truth in Ibsen's *Hedda Gabler* is the same truth-telling as in Sondheim's *Sweeney Todd*. The craft is the same. The biggest difference in a musical is that you must be able to tell the story through song and dance, and that is a matter of study. You want it? Get a great singing teacher and go to dance class every day! For singing, I highly recommend the amazing Heather Petruzelli.

NOTE:

Contradictions

Look for contradictions as you organize your character traits. It builds internal conflict which is particularly wonderful on camera. For instance, a sweet, kind priest may also have a raging temper when inebriated. I recently directed the marvelous Shami McCormick in Neil Simon's classic, *Lost in Yonkers*. She played the terrifying Grandmother Kurnitz. The two young boys in the script were rightfully terrified of her, but at the end of the show they had survived her tyranny. As the boys left their grandmother's apartment for the last time, you could see a moment of pure sweetness wash across Shami's face. The audience never saw it coming and it enriched her creation. It made the performance that much more complicated. Look for ambivalence. It adds poetry and heightens the humanity.

NOTE:
The Advertising Game

The beauty of union television and film gigs is the magic of the residual. A residual is a payment that the performer receives EVERY time her movie, commercial, or TV show airs. The residual is built into the contract. It was negotiated years ago to protect the performer and it is a wonderful thing. So, every time you see another *Abbot Elementary* on TV, take comfort knowing all those actors are getting richer! Trust me, that is why so many actors are hustling for this kind of work.

For commercials and voice-over work, take a class. These disciplines take much more time and space than I have here. My beloved friend, Joan See, wrote the best book on commercials: *Acting in Commercials: A Guide to Auditioning and Performing on Camera*. Study it.

Every producer and director I've worked with in commercials, TV, film, and voice-over work wants choices. So, give them your choices first then be prepared to offer at least three different reads or takes.

Here's how to accomplish that:

- Change the back-story or relationship.
- Change the genre, i.e., from sitcom to documentary.
- Use a different intention.
- Stress other operative words.
- Switch the tempo.
- Change your eye focus.

- Deliver the text to a different imaginary person.
- Smile, frown, laugh.
- Use a different pitch range.
- Change the tone. If it's soft, make it edgy.

NOTE:

Voice and Speech

Great actors easily transition from stage to screen. They can fill an eight-hundred-seat theatre as easily as they work with cutting-edge amplification on a film set. These artists can calibrate their vocal and articulation choices to fit the medium. A working understanding of flexible speech is needed not just for clarity, but also to create believable accents for the stage and camera. An instrument that can play only a few notes severely limits your ability to make a solid living. There is a lot of work out there, more now than ever: voice-overs, webisodes, animation, stage, camera and more. However, the technique for work in each of these areas is different and engages a skill set that must be developed. The best teacher for it is my mentor, Louis Colaianni. He is the finest voice and speech teacher I know.

NOTE:

The Camera Never Lies

The medium determines the color palette of your acting choices. In film, those choices aren't smaller, but they are different. We go to the theatre to hear a play; we go to the cinema to see a movie. It's the editor's and director's art form—their choices determine our performances. So, a working knowledge of what the shot is, the frame of the screen and how to calibrate vocal and physical action on camera will lead to valuable screen time.

On camera work is a poker game. The camera loves behavior, so don't rush your reactions or feel you need to push the pace unless the material calls for it (as in the quickly paced comedy, *The Marvelous Mrs. Maisel*). Your job in film is to give the editor material—something he or she can cut to and mold. Next time you watch a movie, study the actors' reactions, and watch for subtle pauses they take before speaking. A loaded pause speaks volumes.

Don't wait to respond to the end of a thought coming at you to react. People are not polite. React early. React to any stimulus on your partner's line without upstaging them. And for the stage physicalize your reactions (subtly). For the camera, allow the adjustments to wash through your eyes—off the text. Each moment offers three stories: The initial reaction, the dialogue, and the final remark. The stage allows volcanic eruptions, full-throated with enormous volume. The camera demands the quiet simmer.

NOTE:
Line, Please

There are many ways to commit the script to memory. I will share all the ways I have learned. However, everyone learns differently. The lucky few who have photographic memories never worry.

The most important help I can give you is to learn your lines out loud using full voice. You want to build a muscle memory in your mouth, tongue, teeth, and lips. Think of it as learning a word dance.

Memorize thoughts, not lines. There may be two thoughts in one sentence or three sentences may make one complicated thought. Break your script down into thoughts, not grammar. Writers use punctuation, human beings don't use punctuation. They use impulse.

WRITE YOUR LINES DOWN IN
LONGHAND. REPEAT.

RECORD YOUR LINES ON
YOUR PHONE. REPEAT.

RECORD ONLY YOUR CUES ON
YOUR PHONE. REPEAT.

TAKE A THOUGHT AND SAY IT OUT LOUD
TEN TIMES. THEN ADD MORE THOUGHTS.

ASK SOMEONE WHO TRULY LOVES YOU
TO RUN THE LINES WITH YOU!
Running lines can be very boring
so it helps if they love you!

WHEN NOT EMPLOYED, LEARN A
SHAKESPEARE SONNET EVERY WEEK.

WHEN IN DOUBT, GOOGLE IT!
The Internet has many apps that you can
utilize to help memorize your lines.

NOTE:
Nothing To Cry About

There will come a time when you will play a role that demands tears. Either another character will say to you, "Don't cry" or in the next scene, someone will refer to you blubbering at the ballet. Nothing to be done. It's an obligation. Must cry. Just have to. As a young actor, I was amazed by the gift of real tears onstage. I have played long runs and cried real tears every night. I have had long runs and cried real tears 75 percent of the time even though I changed nothing in my preparation. Sometimes, it just didn't happen though everything else about my performance was exactly the same. My tone of voice, the words, my posture, the blocking—all the same but no tears. I learned from my coach Louis that it was my breathing that was not dropped in. *Dropped in* means that you are taking a full unrestricted breath from deep in your center. Without a released breath, a relaxed jaw, an open throat, and loose tongue, the tears will be constricted. Think what happens when we actually cry. When we suppress tears, our breath constricts, our tongue tightens up, and our jaw locks. Anything to keep from weeping. Yes, that is fine in real life when you want to avoid appearing weak or being humiliated, but in front of the camera for fifteen takes or on stage for eight shows a week in a nine-month extended run, it just won't work. Here we must discuss the difference between reality and craft.

Your rehearsal tears may be real but if you cannot repeat them on cue then they are not craft, they're an accident. Acting requires precision. Repeatable tears are a by-product of the good work you have done in creating character and playing the truth of the scene. To facilitate tears (or any large emotion) your physical instrument must be free. Your body, acting, and the breath must function as a whole.

That said, it's worth repeating Sandford Meisner's joke about tears. A student was begging him for the secret to tears and finally Meisner, one of the world's greatest acting teachers replied, "Don't worry, you'll get there. But just remember that if tears were talent, my Aunt Tilly would have an Oscar!"

NOTE:
Readings

It is now the form to gather actors, producers, and money people together to read a play or screenplay. A test-run of sorts. I've done well over a hundred of them. It's cheap, quick and helpful. It can lead to work for an actor and helps build your reputation within the industry. There are staged readings with rough blocking and straight reads at a table.

I recently took part in a reading for backers that starred Mandy Patinkin, of *Homeland* fame. Austin Pendleton directed and Hal Prince produced it at The Directors Company in New York City. Oh, and not for nothing, but the cast also featured the luminous Blythe Danner (Broadway royalty), and my friend, the supremely talented Tony winner, Reed Birney. The play was a lovely slice of life, a bittersweet comedy by Joanna Glass. We assembled to read the challenging text for a theatre full of potential producers and artistic directors. No "How are you? Have a coffee." Nothing. Sit down and read the damn thing.

I was sweating. I learned a lesson that day that only a seasoned artist like Patinkin can teach. He had several long speeches to deliver, and he also had a shooting schedule for *Homeland* to negotiate. But for the fact that Hal Prince was attached, we'd never have had Mandy. Halfway through the second act, in the middle of a seemingly obvious moment of exposition, Mandy Patinkin broke. Tears flooded his eyes and all the air went out of the room. The audience and the actors (including me) were utterly shocked by his commitment. With all of those impediments to his time, Mandy Patinkin, Tony winner, gave all he had to the writing of this wonderful play. He didn't judge it. He was all in and consequently brought real magic to the reading. I'll never forget it. I recently watched a clip of the great violinist Itzhak Perlman playing "Take Me Out to the Ball Game" at Citi Field. He did it with as much passion as if it were a Bach concerto. Great artists don't judge the work.

Lesson: serve the playwright; serve the work. It's not about how clever you are. Stick to the script. Do NOT improvise the writing or add pauses to places that the writer has not put them. Do your homework. You are there to serve the playwright's vision. Your honest, clean read is your sole purpose. In a four-week rehearsal, you can get interesting, but for a reading. it's the writer who is the star. Remember, few of us ever get to be "the star"; writers less so than others. Oh, and have a bag full of resumes, get the names of everyone in the room and send them thank you notes!

CAREER NOTES

NOTE:
The Business

YOUR CAREER IS NOT A SPRINT, it's a marathon. Your primary job is to meet contacts, build a base of friends, fans, and industry professionals, and to cultivate these relationships. It's an old saying but truer now than ever: "It's not what you know, it's who you know." And do all of these people know where you are and how to contact you at every minute of the day? I have lost jobs because I just couldn't be found. It's a horrible feeling. Once, right out of college, my roommate failed to pass on the message of a paying gig for me. I still feel the pain. So don't drop the ball; casting happens at warp speed.

It may take years of networking and cultivation before your diligence bears fruit. I have worked for the wonderful D. Lynn Myers at Ensemble Theatre of Cincinnati several times, but it took me nearly twenty years to be cast. I first met Ms. Myers in 1985. I was on tour with a children's show (our daily stipend for food was $7) and as we passed through Cincinnati, I set up a courtesy audition with her. There are many times when just by asking a regional theatre if they have time to see you, they will. It's a form of courtesy to offer the actor ten minutes, but it's all in the timing. If the theatre is in tech week, probably not (but you might get lucky). It does not hurt to ask. Sometimes all it takes is the guts to send a text. Remember, you are also helping them.

I met with Ms. Myers, did my two contrasting monologues. She was as gracious a theatre professional as I had ever met. She proved a point that I learned very late in my career: Actors are the lifeblood of the casting office. D. Lynn wanted me to be good. She was aching for fresh talent. Seeing me do my monologues was as much for her theatre as it was for my career.

I didn't get the job that day, but I kept in touch with D. Lynn for twenty years. A note every six months:

> Hi, how are you?
> I just finished a gig at The Hangar Theatre playing "Gabe" in *Dinner With Friends*. I'm free in the fall and I see you're doing *Stones in His Pockets*. I'd love to read for you.
> Best, Chris

Every Christmas, a card; the occasional opening night congratulatory note and if I could, of course, I'd see one of her productions. I certainly worked that contact. I knew she was a player the minute we met and I never forgot her enthusiasm. It worked. She remembered me. I was cast in that production of *Stones in His Pockets*; the following season in *Sight Unseen*; the season after in *Good People*. Three wonderful gigs. It took many years, but I finally made some money. It's a marathon. The money will come but you have to play the long game. I often say the best way to have a career in the entertainment industry is not to quit.

Remember, all great casting directors (CDs) are constantly looking for interesting actors. That might not be readily apparent. For years, I read their shortness with me as rejection when it was just the stress of their intense profession. They know it's a marathon. They know that the skinny, Italian kid with the sweet *Awake and Sing* monologue from Pittsburgh may not be right for today's gig, but is perfect for the new Lin Manuel Miranda musical they're producing eight months from now. From my twenty-five years as a professional director on the other side of the audition table, I can also tell you that although we auditors may seem grumpy, hungry, and distracted (we often are), we are also actually praying that your sixteen bars blow our minds and that we have found the perfect Hamilton. I've seen bitter, cynical producers cursing their decision to ever work in the theatre one minute, jump out of their seats the next and pump the hand of the actor who just wowed the room as if he were their prospective son-in-law. It's called relief. A moment earlier, what we'd all been thinking was, "What if we don't find our Alexander Hamilton? How much more time and money will we need for further casting?"

Write letters. You'll stand out. Of course, Instagram, Facebook and Twitter are today's standard modes of communication. However, that's why a handwritten "thank you" note stands out. Invest in personal stationery and follow up your meetings with a thank you note. Send a card every six months advertising your latest gigs. Believe me, you will stand out. And if someone emails you congratulating you on your work, acknowledge it. Sometimes your only pay is recognition.

Make sure everyone who could possibly cast you has your contact information. This means, agents, casting directors, casting assistants, directors, networks, advertising agencies and professional stage managers.

NOTE:
Chops

Keep your chops (skills) sharp by continuing to study the craft. Seek out the great teachers and make a name for yourself in their class. It's the best way to keep your finger on the pulse of the casting world. Your classmates will often help you get an audition, your teacher will have contacts for you as well, and of course, you'll be that much closer to becoming a master. Remember the ten thousand hours?

NOTE:
Reputation

Good work, professionalism, preparation, integrity, and flexibility build your reputation. However, bad behavior in rehearsals, a missed show, drinking on the job, changing blocking, bullying cast mates (or worse molesting them), all lead to a rap that stains your resume and will eventually lead to a life of bussing tables or incarceration. There is almost no way to re-do your reputation. A bad reputation spreads like the plague. A good reputation begins the minute you walk into the audition room. You really don't have a second chance to make a good first impression. Your integrity is built by doing what you say you will and being where you say you will at the appointed time. Warning: you are not going to like all the people you work with in this field. Temperamental artists can be a pain and the more famous they are the more challenging they may seem. It's your job to grin and bear it. Keep your wits about you. Breathe and smile. Then go home, call a confidante, and vent safely.

NOTE:

Preparation

The wildly talented Kate Hampton taught me a wonderful technique. As I was coaching her for the Broadway production of *Harry Potter and the Cursed Child*, I noticed a series of hash marks on the front of her script. She does that to track her prep. She rehearses her audition sides fifty times before going into the room. It pays off as she frequently works on Broadway and on TV.

NOTE:

Friends

Today, friends are counted in thousands and follow us on Instagram and Twitter. Many agents, managers, and producers are not so interested in how you handle iambic pentameter as they are in how many followers you have; numbers are very attractive to producers and network heads. Followers mean butts in the seats. In today's competitive entertainment world, if you can help the marketing division with your presence on social media, it may get you a job. My young friend Isaiah Stannard has a principle role on NBC's *Good Girls*. The first thing the executives in Los Angeles said to him was that it's MANDATORY to harness thousands of followers on social media. In fact, pay raises are often based on increased numbers of followers. Don't wait for the suits to tell you that, start now. Document your acting life daily. Make it a game, be creative and announce to the world that you are their next big thing. It's a challenge to the introverted (many of our greatest actors are introverts), but it is the new standard of networking. Play or get out. No one made you be an actor. If self-promotion is distasteful to you, I respect that, but you need to advocate for yourself.

Good friends are vital. They make our lives bearable when the career is failing and our celebrations richer when things are going well. I have helped many friends get jobs, very often in projects that I'm not even directing. Here's a case in point. A desperate fellow director once called me at two in the morning in tears. She was looking to fill the role of Mercutio for a production in Toledo. Did I know anyone? Reliable? Plays well with others? Fast study? "Yeah, call this guy." We all must pay it forward. I'm sure she will save my ass some day and if she doesn't, I've done a good deed. The show must go on, and I'll do anything for that to happen—for anyone. It's our community, our duty, our integrity.

My son was two years old. I had not left town for regional work since his birth but needed money badly. My beloved friend Wynn, called me in a froth one afternoon and let me know that he had just been cast as Freddie in the classic comedy, *Noises Off* at Indiana Rep. He had overheard the producers and the brilliant director, Risa Brainin, bemoaning the fact that they could not find a suitable Lloyd (the director of the play within the play). Wynn let them know that I was their guy. (I had directed Wynn in several shows at The Depot Theatre, and he knew I had the right touch for the part.) I called my agent, he set up my slot for the next morning and I crammed the thirteen pages. I booked the job. We all looked good. Wynn for solving their casting dilemma, the director for crafting a superlative show, and me for acting it well.

Years later, my dear friend and mentor, Louis Colaianni

bought me an everything bagel with nova and red onion at Murray's on Eighth Avenue. Murray's is the perfect place in NYC for theatre folk to make deals. The best deals, after all, are always done over heavy Jewish food: blintzes, bagels, borscht. All New Yorkers are Jewish even if they received Holy Communion at Saint Vitus Church.

Louis knew that I was struggling to make ends meet; had dedicated my life to the entertainment industry but was still living on rice and beans and pushing fifty. (Even the best of our efforts don't always put bread on the table). He offered to train me to teach the Linklater voice method for the stage, but it was expensive. Thousands of dollars expensive. I hardly had the two bucks for the subway home. However, I needed to act fast or I was going to have to leave my dreams behind, move back to Pittsburgh, and sell used cars for a living. I'm not kidding. Dear, kind Louis said that he wanted me to have enough money in my pocket to afford a coffee. He also said that the money I spent on our training would come back to me many times over. It was a leap. An expensive leap. I wiped the cream cheese from my face, swallowed hard and leapt. He was right. The training has made me thousands of dollars. I've taught the Linklater Method all over the country and it's been the springboard to a successful career as an educator.

It's not a sprint, it's a marathon. There are times when you need to reassess and take a new road. The lesson: keep your friends close to your heart. Beware the dark ones who can find no light in their careers. They can drag you down. Love them, but don't get sucked into their negative game.

NOTE:

Money, Money, Money

The prevailing sentiment around money in the acting industry is that performers rarely make very much of it. I was repeatedly told that I would starve if I followed my passion to act, and so I believed it. However, the truth is many actors do quite well and lead financially healthy lives. It takes skill but is a very real possibility. To stay the course, develop a realistic budget and stick to it. Knowing what your life actually costs to run each month and what you value (expensive dinners or great resume photographs?) will keep you in the game. Also, when you are acting, put 30% of your take-home pay away to subsidize your life when you are not working. Think long term rather than check to check. As I said at the outset of the book, your career is a marathon, not a sprint.

NOTE:

Unemployment

Stephen Colbert said that when you're working, you feel like you'll always work and when you're unemployed, you're certain that you'll always be unemployed. Not working as an actor can have a damaging effect on even the healthiest ego. I've known brilliant actors, true artists, who left the business after a handful of failed auditions. They just couldn't stomach the idea that rejection would be a part of their everyday existence. It is existential: I fail;

therefore, I am an actor. Eventually, there can be a tipping point. In an art form that is based on sharing your soul with strangers in a cold room, it is fair for you to ask, "is this how I want to spend my energy? Do I have the guts to survive these spiritual slings and arrows?"

Now add to the equation that you are being rejected for jobs that pay such a meager wage that it requires you to pick up yet another part-time gig passing out Little Caesar's flyers to afford it. Acting is a selfish business. I have been fired from countless survival gigs. I'd book a play, pick up a new survival job, keep it until I didn't need it and get fired or simply quit. I'm not proud of this history but something had to give. You must look out for yourself even if you have Creative Artists Agency making your calls.

No one made me choose the entertainment industry and staying in still requires perseverance. The Civil Rights Movement had the perfect motto: "Keep your eyes on the prize." There are also hundreds of self-help success manuals out there but none for actors. The successful business leader or tech genius who pens these guides could never ever understand the difference between selling cars and selling yourself. Never get it. Not for a minute. The pain, the courage of putting yourself out there is enormous.

My only advice is to find a balance. Keep friends close, avoid alcohol and drugs and toxic relationships, and do something every day that makes you feel like an artist. Go to the movies, read a new author, write a monologue, bring friends together to read *Hamlet*, learn a sonnet, take a class, create your own gigs. Always "keep your eyes on the prize"—a creative life you can be proud of that is rich with friends. After many years, I have found my mission statement: to work on interesting material with interesting people. Write your own. The very act of writing it is the first step in bringing it to life.

NOTE:
Cup of Tea

I have had great auditions. Played my heart out and believed I was certainly in the running for a callback; pumped up like a tick, pleased with my genius only to encounter a table full of people bored to death. They were quietly checking their X (formerly Twitter) feed while I was laying bare my soul. What happened? Was I right or were they? If you play it honestly and execute your audition well, leave it at that. You will not be everyone's cup of tea. You must be willing to risk rejection at the price of being authentic. That's the cold reality of auditions. But the next audition may be the opposite experience; they just love you! It's a numbers game. Pick up your head, thank the table, go home, study this chapter of the book and move on to your next opportunity.

I love this quote from the brilliant Jason Bateman. He has had plenty of success and failure, which has left him with a sobering view of auditions. On being cast in *Arrested Development*, he said, "I guessed right that day and did what they were looking for." Sometimes it's that simple and that maddening.

THE PATH TO THE ROOM
Right This Way...

NOTE:
Auditions

Auditions can be awful, but you've got to learn to love them. Unless you become a household name, you will be auditioning for the rest of your life. I have personally auditioned over a thousand times and witnessed well over two thousand auditions. Let's discuss.

This is how most jobs that you'll audition for become auditions. To begin, there will be a script, a play, a teleplay, or screenplay. Here are the players: at the top is a producer or many producers. They are responsible for finding the right material and putting the money together. They will hire a support team that consists of director, designers, technicians and casting directors. After many days of creative discussions, the director will confer with the casting director and draw up a breakdown (a description of the roles to be cast) for each character. The breakdown will read something like this:

HAMLET: We are seeking a male or female actor with extraordinary language skills with stage combat experience to play the title role in The Alabama Shakespeare Festival's production of *Hamlet* slated for October 2021. Actor must be very funny, athletic, and able to handle the intellectual and physical demands of the text. All ethnic types are requested.

The CD then will send the breakdowns to theatrical agents and managers. (A manager is like an agent but their fees are higher. Unless you're a huge star, stick with agents. They work just as hard and charge less.) The agent submits a set of pictures and resumes of those clients he or she believes are right for the role. The director and producer will have a short list that will be considered as well.

Once all the submissions are in, (several hundred by the way), the CD will choose the twenty to read for the role. And you, lucky actor, get the call time and material for the audition and essentially apply for the job or "read for the role". The audition is not opening night, but it does reflect hours of preparation. So how do those twenty get chosen? First, the resume must show that they have the chops necessary to handle heightened poetic language. The resume must also list real fight skills and at least one comedic role.

Furthermore, it improves their chances if the actor has carried a show—that is, played a big lead in a challenging show. The pressure of carrying a play is intense. It makes all the stakeholders feel better if they know that that same actor they're bringing in to audition played Lady Macbeth last summer at The Pennsylvania Shakespeare Festival. However, without an agent, the physically gifted actor with great intelligence, classical chops, and comedic skills won't get seen for the role. Lose no faith friends. There are still "open calls". More on those later.

NOTE:
Catch-22

Joseph Heller wrote a novel called *Catch-22*. A "catch-22" is a simple but maddening paradox. In the novel, an air force pilot, terrified of dying, tries to be discharged on the grounds that he is crazy and unfit for duty. His commanding officer maintains that if he were truly crazy he wouldn't know it, and he'd still fly. The fact that he wanted to stop killing Germans proved he was not mad, but sane. Hence, a catch-22. The same paradox applies to getting an agent. You'll hear at least a hundred times a day, "That audition is closed" and that "They are only seeing agents' submissions" for a role for which you are perfect. So, you need an agent to be submitted but first, you need an agent. Catch-22. It's enough to make a young actor quit.

NOTE:
So How Do You Get One?

Some BFA and MFA programs culminate in a student showcase in NYC, Chicago, and LA. Agents will be all too happy to sign you for a contract if you bring the goods. Each spring, hundreds of talented actors find agents by way of these showcases.

Other ways to be seen and signed by agents:

1. Perform with Improv groups. Agents love comedians. All of *SNL* comes from Improv groups.

2. Ask friends for an introduction. If you're in a show, beg your friend to bribe their agent to see it and you. I got a great agent that way.

3. Research the agents, then send them your stuff with a great letter. There are online guides and information for every agent. Do your homework.

4. Find an agent in a smaller market. It's easier. Live in NYC but need an agent? Find one in Boston or Philly or Atlanta. They are just a bus ride away and with the advent of self-tape, what does it matter where you or your agent lives?

5. Apprentice in an agent's office. It's a great way to show them how smart, funny, and diligent you are—ask to be seen.

6. Ask a casting director for help. If you have a good relationship with a casting director, ask her to introduce you to an agent. Casting directors deal with agents every day. They listen to each other.

7. Be a scene reader. The best way to build a relationship with a casting director is to work as a reader for them. A reader is the actor in the audition studio who "reads" the other lines in the scene for the auditioning actor. It's a great way to show off your skills, especially as you may be reading several roles. Watch twenty actors make the same mistake and I assure you, you won't make that same mistake when it's your turn to audition.

8. Build a reel. Shoot scenes on your iPhone and cut it together like a series of short scenes. What does it matter that they're not from a feature film? A rep only needs to know what you look and sound like on camera.

9. Pay to play. There are businesses in LA and NYC that bring in casting directors, agents, managers, and producers that an actor can pay to meet and read for. The Actors Connection, One on One NYC, and Next Level Studios LA are examples, but choose wisely as those fees will add up.

10. Create your own work. Get your friends together and do a play or shoot a web series. Create a podcast. Get creative! Unemployment is the mother of creation!

Open calls are auditions available to any actor motivated enough to show up early and sign in. There are both union and non-union open calls. Union calls now have slots at the end of the day for non-union actors. It takes persistence and grit, but this is the work. It's not glamorous, but it can lead to employment. That work leads to a showcase for the actor, who can then sell the show to agents. That open call can secure representation. So, get out of bed and log into the site! These calls are advertised each week on several websites and through the unions. I, myself, have landed three excellent gigs by standing in line and offering up my two-minute comedic monologue, and I've made deep and profitable relationships with dozens of theatres, producers and casting directors at open calls. (It's called paying your dues.) Everyone is looking for the next great thing, and so it matters not whether they find you through an agent submission or an open call.

NOTE:
Unions: Actors' Rights

Founded in 1913, the Actors' Equity Association (AEA) is the trade union that protects stage actors and stage managers. At some point, the serious actor must join its ranks. Sadly, unions have been given a bad name—mostly because the world doesn't really know what they do for their members and why they came into existence in the first place. Without unions, capitalism would run roughshod over the American actor. Before Actors' Equity Association was organized, actors were on their own and subject to dangerous and inhumane working conditions. AEA was founded to negotiate with producers and theatres regarding work hours, working conditions, benefits, and salaries. Trust me, good reader, without a union the producers would not treat you well at all. To us, the theatre is more than just a job, it is an art form; to them, it's a dollars and cents game. If producers had the chance to make more money by running a show twelve times a week and killing the cast, they'd do it in a heartbeat.

The other acting union is the Screen Actors Guild/American Federation of Television and Radio Artists. SAG covers film actors and AFTRA covers work in television and radio.

You may purchase your SAG/AFTRA card anytime you like and now, with Open Access, you may join AEA in similar fashion. Here is the boilerplate verbiage from The AEA website:

> *You may join Equity under the "Open Access" program if you have worked professionally as an actor or stage manager in a theatrical production within Equity's geographical jurisdiction. If you have worked on a previous Equity Contract, worked as an Equity Membership Candidate or Local Jobber or have been a member of Equity prior you may contact us to inquire about joining and filing a new Membership Application.*
>
> *If you have worked professionally as an actor or stage manager in Equity's geographical jurisdiction, you will need to provide a copy of your contract and proof of earnings (i.e. pay stub, W2, 1099, etc.). If you are join*

ing Equity through Open Access, at least a $600 initial payment is due with your application. You must also prove that you have been paid for some of your theatre work.

Beware of joining a union too soon in your career as it puts you in competition with much more seasoned actors. I believe it's wise to book many non-union gigs to learn the rules and build a strong audition reel (video clips of yourself) and then join. Of course, all bets are off if someone offers you a union gig! When that happens, sign the contract!

YOU GOT IN THE ROOM
Now What?

NOTE:
Monologue Auditions

FOR MONOLOGUE AUDITIONS, choose material that suits your type and talents. Your "type" is the kind of role(s) the industry sees you as being right for—something you'd be cast in (more on this later). Yes, I know, you long to play Dumbledore but it makes no sense to bring you in if you're twenty-three years old!

Your choice of monologue tells me a lot. With thousands of monologues to choose from, pick one that highlights your talents. If you're witty, pick Oscar Wilde; poetic and period, August Wilson; eloquent, Shakespeare. I hate crying and kicking and screaming pieces. It's just too much for me to take in. Furthermore, your primary piece should be something you could do in an agent's office or in a close-up. There will be times when you are asked, "What else can you show us?" Be prepared. This is a chance to show off all those hours of preparation. Give them choices. Have other monologues ready. If you need contrasting monologues, one has to be funny. Not mildly amusing—downright funny. Have a Shakespeare piece ready.

If you sing, have songs that tell a story and that show your vocal range. As with monologues, have several songs of different genres available. If a song that you like isn't in your vocal range, have it transposed. Don't ask the accompanist to do it on the fly. Make sure your music is clearly marked and easy for the accompanist to follow. Most people put their song pages back-to-back, slip them into clear sheet protectors, and put them in a three-ring binder to make page turning easy. Give any instructions to the accompanist politely and thank them before you leave the room.

NOTE:
Time and Patience

It is the rare audition that runs on time. Invariably, the auditors run behind and a wave of panic will overtake the whole process. Actors in the holding room will start worrying about their next appointment; lunches will be skipped. It gets ugly. Don't allow the time crunch to interfere with your audition. Don't let it happen. Do your work. Here's how. Once the room is yours, take a few seconds to create the moment before the scene/monologue begins, breathe in the stimulus that makes you behave or speak your first line. The first word of your monologue is not the beginning of your audition. The beginning is reacting to the conjured action from your imaginary scene partner that makes YOU do or say something. Do not rush this step. Remember, the moment and the stage are yours—be there; own it.

NOTE:
Build a Bridge

Do your research. If you've seen a show the director has done or worked with an actor the theatre loves (be sure about this latter) and you sense the moment in the room is right, then build your bridge. Drop a quick: "I saw your Tempest last season. It was amazing" or "I studied with Carole at NYU. She's great." Go further. Ask them questions. People love to talk about themselves. If you learn to ask open-ended questions, you'll be a hit at the audition as well as the cocktail circuit and remembered long after your last note. Make your time in the room special.

NOTE:
Be Yourself

I'm not looking for somebody else. This requires that you be true to yourself and understand your taste, politics, faith, passion and while honoring the text, add your particular spin on the read (your rosin.). There is plenty about the business of auditioning which is out of your control. However, the preparation you bring to the text and character as well as your professional demeanor and focus are well within your control. The brilliant Julianne Moore said that when she auditions she does exactly what she wants, what she thinks of the character because she knows once she hits the set, it will most likely be out of her hands.

The auditors, of course, want to know if you are right for the part but also if they will enjoy working with you for the next eight weeks.

NOTE:
Professional Standards

The professional standard in auditions today is to be off-book (fully memorized) for casting sessions.

NOTE:
The Slate

The slate is the announcement of your monologues or songs. For example, "I will be doing Ophelia from *Hamlet*, and singing "Popular" from *Wicked*." Rehearse this as much as your acting. Present the slate with joy and clean articulation.

NOTE:

Monologue Focus

For monologue auditions, don't look at the auditors unless we request it. As a director, the last thing I want to do is act all day with those auditioning. Keep your focus just above the auditors' heads.

NOTE:

Make a Choice

As I laid out earlier in the technique portion of the book, you must be crystal clear about the story you're telling. In auditions that work from scenes or sides, this is particularly important. Read the entire play! Be clear about your take on the character and reflect that perspective. This is known as "making a choice." It may seem daunting at first, having to commit to a story. A risk, yes, but one that will distinguish you. It will also anchor your audition. This choice, (Hamlet wants to bring his family back together) is your take on the material. Sure, you can go in the room and play it just as yourself. Don't get me wrong. Bringing yourself to the role is necessary but more importantly, what story from the play are you telling? Determining and committing to your answer can separate you from the other nineteen women in the holding room. A director will never fault you for making a storytelling choice. On the contrary, they will be grateful to you for offering your opinion on the material. I've seen hundreds of actors make the same choice in reading for a role only to lose the job because they failed to extrovert the dramatic action and their character's place in it. So, READ the DAMN script! "Oh! Hamlet dies in the end? Wish I had known that!" If you can't read the script, read as many reviews of the playwright's work and interviews with her as Google offers. Get to know what makes the writer tick. Finally, think about why the theatre chose her play to open their 25th season.

NOTE:
Know Your Type

Compile a list of roles you want to play. Research who is playing those parts and has the career you desire. Do you share similar qualities as the actor(s) getting cast in these good roles? If you are confused about your type, ask your friends and teachers. Are you the best friend or the wise-cracking jokester? The introverted scientist or the dangerous stranger? Knowing how others "type" or see you will help prioritize your auditions. Knowing that you are not the funny middle-aged guy will help you roll with rejection. You will be easier on yourself if you understand what the auditors are seeking for the project. If possible, go see the show that you auditioned for to learn who ultimately got the part. It will clarify the process.

NOTE:
Reaction to Direction in the Audition

A director may give you an adjustment to make during the audition. Certainly feel free to ask a follow-up question if you're confused by the direction. However, if your first reaction is to debate the director's vision, chances are that this will be your last visit with her.

NOTE:
Got Questions?

You don't have to ask questions, but if something is unclear or throwing you off about the character or play, do so. But for God's sake, be brief and succinct. I had an actor once say to me, "Is she married to this guy?" If she had simply read the script we sent a week earlier, she would have known that the characters were brother and sister. Did I mention read the play?

NOTE:
Never Apologize.

You may have been great in an audition, but you thought you crashed. The auditors may think you were terrific. If you tell them you sucked, you may undermine their positive opinion of you. It may insult their intelligence. It also feels like a passive-aggressive way of fishing for a compliment. To me, it makes you come off as needy and overly focused on your ego. In either case,

I may reconsider hiring you because your neediness might slow down the process. So, don't apologize! Smile, offer your thanks, stride brilliantly out of the room, THEN beat yourself up!

NOTE:

The Entrance

What do you say with your entrance? "I'm terrified. I'm racing. I'm a mess. I don't want to be here?" Or are you thrilled to share your work, to play? Those first few seconds can help you book the job. If you're a mess, it worries me. "Is he going to be responsible for the next eight weeks? If he's a mess now, what will rehearsal and opening night be like?" To avoid the mess, plan to be an extra half hour early. Furthermore, you don't want to run to a call back. The very act of running releases stress hormones and additional stress won't do your audition any favors. Don't bring your personal crisis or frustrations into the audition with you. Recently, an actor burst into the room like a maniac. I never got over his rage walking in to read. Afterward, the super-talented casting director, Gayle Seay, said she never got over it either. He was so aggressive that none of us wanted to work with him.

NOTE:

Baggage

Purses, backpacks, overcoats—leave them by the door and take them with you when you leave. You'll never forget it. Nothing worse than having to come back in and sheepishly retrieve it. Not a strong exit. Warning: do not leave valuables in the waiting room. If you suddenly think I left my laptop in the hall in the middle of your audition, you're sunk.

NOTE:

P & R's

Bring a few extra hard copies of your picture and resume to your audition. We may have lost it or the internet is down or there may be another director in the room who'd like it for her files. Have it close at hand. Digging through your gigantic bag is no fun to watch.

NOTE:

Sides

If you are given sides (a few pages from the script) and there is more on the page than your lines, study that too. There may be a morsel of text in there that can help you better understand your character and formulate your audition.

NOTE:

Power of "No"

If the people in the room make you feel unsafe or weird, you have the right to excuse yourself from the room or to not take the job. An actor's only power is to say no.

NOTE:
Tattoos & Piercings

Unless you're reading for an ex-con, cover up your tattoos. Remove piercings. I recently sat next to an artistic director who could not get over the piercings. It may seem unfair, but if the character would not be pierced, why muddy the waters? Give yourself the best chance to get the job.

NOTE:
Accounting

Note who was in the room, what the project and role were, and your response to the audition. I've had actors that I have auditioned many times that walk in and have no recollection they had met me before. It's a personal business. Treat it as such.

NOTE:
Think of Auditions as Great Rehearsals

As a young actor, I made the mistake of just bringing in what I did at home. I was frozen into my approach. As I got better at auditioning, I realized that the truly great auditions were just like a wonderful rehearsal where you learned something new about your character or executed a moment in a fresh way. Then, if you don't get the job, you can still feel good about your work. You created something!

NOTE:
The Odds: 1 in 10

Keep auditioning. When I was on the commercial circuit I went through a very dry spell even though I felt I was auditioning well. It happens to the best of us. What was the problem? I spoke to my wonderful agent, Carrie Morgan, and she let me know that I was the second choice on my last seven auditions, which meant I was very good and very close. Still, it wasn't putting bread on my table. She suggested I take a private coaching session with the foremost authority on commercial acting, Joan See. Her book, *Acting in Commercials: A Guide to Auditioning and Performing on Camera,* is still the definitive guide. One hour with Joan and I felt like a new actor. Joan got to the heart of my problem (she thought it was psychological; that I was judging the material, that it was beneath me in some way) and the very next audition, I booked! So, keep auditioning. If you find yourself deeply frustrated or blocked, then it's wise to find a coach. How to do that? Keep your ears open at auditions, enlist the help of others who have good coaches, query your friends. I suggest coaches who are acting teachers rather than casting directors, agents, or managers. There is nothing wrong with that list, but they may not know how actors actually work. An agent knows negotiations but may not understand acting at all. They know results when they see them but may not be able to speak to the process. Yes, there is a fee for coaching, but it's part of doing business in the professional world.

NOTE:
Directors & Producers

Directors and producers are under an enormous amount of stress. It's a business and their livelihood depends on good casting. That same poor director knows all too well his limitations, so his desire to cast well is enormous. We're counting on you to save our work. I can't tell you how many times I've cast well and simply watched the gifted actor work her magic. The venerable Mike Nichols said, "I don't direct films, I cast them."

NOTE:
Don't Listen to Other Actors Auditioning.

Sometimes it's difficult to block out other actors' auditions, especially when everyone is tightly packed into a narrow hallway like cattle (hence the term "cattle calls"). However, do all you can not to listen. Others may be yelling a line where you planned to speak it quietly, and suddenly, you're doubting your Do everything you can to stay focused (free, deep breaths are great for this; so are earplugs). By the time you are actually called into read for the role, you will have made your choices. Trust them. If you change horses mid-stream, disaster and frustration await.

NOTE:
The Holding Room

It's painfully ironic that many times the holding rooms at Ripley-Grier Studios in New York City resemble the emergency room at Bellevue Hospital on a Saturday night. Instead of bleeding and hacking desperate patients; it's sweating and mumbling desperate actors. What's the difference? On the other hand, the waiting room can feel like a class reunion. Sure, it's wonderful to see your long-lost friends from summer stock, but that's not the energy for your audition. Just protect yourself and honor the work. Moreover, it's rude to distract someone who is trying to prep. Just shut up until after. Tom Bloom is a perennial Broadway actor, and you have seen him countless times on TV. I recently ran into him on the subway. We spoke for a few minutes, and then he simply said, "I need to prep now". We were about forty minutes from the studio. There's a reason he works so much. Respect your fellow actors and the craft. Coffee can wait.

NOTE:
Costumes

Unnecessary tension is the death of relaxation and the Achilles' heel of a good audition. Don't risk it. As a seven-year-old Catholic boy, I was taught to lay out my school clothes the night before so I'd be ready for the bus. My mom knew it would cut down on panic. She was right and the same rule applies for actors. The last thing you want to do is rifle through your sweaters for the perfect look. Also, dress with a nod to the part if you can.

A successful actor has dozens of costumes in her wardrobe. A nurse, board president, nun, etc. Avail yourself of The Salvation Army, Goodwill, tag sales. Be ready to walk in as the part. It is sad and greatly discouraging, but many casting directors and producers (particularly in on-camera work) find it difficult to believe you can honestly play a doctor while not dressed in a white lab coat! It's infuriating, but this is an instance where you can moan about the folks making decisions about your career, or you can take action.

Buy some costumes! When I was casting *The Importance of Being Earnest* for Florida Rep, I had a hard time seriously considering one actor who read for the dandified Algernon Moncrief in flip-flops! When auditioning for a classic play, almost anything before 1960, a man should have a jacket and tie and a woman a real dress and proper leather shoes with heels. Clothes determine what physical choices you can execute; the silhouette of a character is something that you can control.

NOTE:
Working with a Costume Designer

I know for a fact that the great designers are eager to know your feelings about the costumes. My go-to designer, Stefanie Genda, always wants to know where the actor is taking the role. She knows that it's a collaboration. The first talks I have with Stephanie are not about color, fabric, or pattern. Yes, that is vital, but what we discuss for hours is who is Blanche? What does she want? What are her fears? And what do the clothes say about her inner story? Are the costumes camouflage or a billboard? As a fellow artist, the key is to respect the designer and still find a way to advocate for your character and your vision.

NOTE:
TV, Film, & Voice-Over Choices

Every producer or director I've worked with in commercials, TV, film, or voice-over work wants choices. So, give them your choice first, then be prepared to offer at least three different reads or takes.

Here's how to accomplish that:

- Change the backstory or the relationship.
- Change the genre, e.g., from sitcom to documentary.
- Use a different intention.
- Stress other operative words.
- Switch the tempo.
- Change your eye focus.
- Deliver it to a different imaginary person.
- Smile, frown, laugh.
- Use a different pitch range.
- Change the tone. If it's soft, make it edgy.

NOTE:
Don't Mess With Props

Props can upstage you. It takes weeks of rehearsal for an actor to make props seem natural and supportive of the moment. You'll kick yourself if you blow a call-back because you dropped your water bottle on a laugh line. If there is a prop needed for the storytelling, mime it. I was once at an audition for a short film on the Mafia where an actor pulled out a gun in the waiting room! Needless to say, we all hit the deck. Please: NO weapons!

NOTE:
Use the Audition Room

You come into the audition studio and there is a chair center stage. Move it, if only eight inches stage right. That was somebody else's set. Make a fresh start. It's like a tiger marking its territory. Also, feel free to use ALL the room: lean against the back wall, look out the window, sit on the piano bench, lie on the floor. This use of space distinguishes your audition from the other fifty.

NOTE:
Pictures

Shop around. Meet your photographer. Is she someone you think you can trust? Will she allow you to be yourself? To flirt, to scare, to share all of your personality? Will she shoot different looks appropriate for stage, screen, and commercials? If not, find one that does. The camera catches the relationship you, the subject, have with the photographer. You want to feel free to allow the camera into your heart.

Do your work on your type. Study the entertainment world, ask your friends and teachers, "Who has your career?" Then dress yourself up in the kind of roles that your career model wears in her movies. Your pictures should cast you in roles you can play right now. If you are great at playing lawyers, then take some shots in a three-piece suit. If you play blue-collar, then put on your denim. The final word is that the pictures must be true to what you actually look like. A glamour shot that took special lights and hours of hair and make-up may be great for your ego, but if you don't actually look like that then it's misleading. At the audition, the auditors will expect someone else to come into the room and your 'real' look will be a disappointment to them.

NOTE:
Resumes

Tell the truth. Don't pad your resume or fabricate special skills to appear more interesting. It's a small world. If you get caught, it's a very bad start! Design your resume so it's clean and easy to read. Keep the font simple and consistent. Most importantly, your resume must have all your current contact information.

NOTE:
Self-Tapes

I find it hateful to ask actors to spend even more money on their careers. God knows, they already have plenty of expenses. However, self-taped auditions are not going away and they really do democratize the casting process. Today, actors from Baltimore can audition for feature films when for years it was only actors in LA or New York. So, in this respect, self-taping is a good thing. I have cast several roles from self-tapes. The key to a successful self-tape is in the lighting and the sound. Consider investing in decent lights and a good microphone. The price may hurt at the front end, but knowing that you will do hundreds of self-tapes, in the end the expense will be worth it. The same advice applies to a DIY voice-over booth. Find a closet or a tiny room where you can put down a clean track without extraneous noise. YouTube and the internet have all the equipment you need to create your home studio.

NOTE:
Play Nice With the Reader

As I've said earlier, the reader is usually another actor who reads every scene with the fifty actors who audition and she works hard! It's a long day of acting full out for eight hours. It's a tough job—hard on your voice and requiring massive energy. A good reader makes my job as the director easier because she knows how to feed the actors without upstaging them. I highly recommend being an audition reader. You'll learn more in a day as a reader than you will in any Intro to Acting class. You'll recognize all the points I'm laying out here, AND you may get cast. I have cast my reader twice for plum gigs. Play the scene honestly with them but act and move on their lines. It's your audition, not theirs, so keep the focus on you. Always physically upstage the reader and turn the page on their lines. It keeps the audition fluid. Be respectful of the reader and don't touch them in any way. Remember, even a good reader may not give you everything you need to play the scene fully. They're only human. Regardless, you must play the scene the way you want it. Thank them at the end of the audition. Side note: obviously, the upstaging works with readers, but once you get to rehearsal, it's no longer acceptable behavior. Upstage the star, and it may be your last day on the job.

NOTE:
Keep the Script in Your Hand

Keep the script in your hand even if you never use it. It reminds the auditors, that you are a work in progress. You may think you're off-book, but there's always a chance you can dry. Nerves have that effect. The script can also be quite handy if used well. The style of auditions today is to be fully memorized. Still, I maintain holding a script just in case.

NOTE:
Obligations

When working from sides, if the script says, *she walks into the room*, then you have an obligation to do it. Even if you have to fake it. He drinks a shot. Then do it. She sits down, then do it. It gives your scenes physical shape and shows you've carefully read the text.

NOTE:
Calibrate Your Vocal Projection

Adjust your vocal projection to the size and acoustics of the room. I've cast actors in tiny studios. If you bellow at me for ten minutes, I really can't watch you work. I'm just checking out. I've passed on actors because they assaulted me with their volume. So, get a sense of the acoustics. You'll only be able to do that at the very beginning when you say hello. Yeah, that's fast but you can do it. For musicals, disregard this note. In a musical audition, your song must be sung as composed

NOTE:
Rehearse With Someone

Rehearse with a good someone. Have them play the scene well. You need to know what forces are coming at you. Processing information is part of every scene. There will be times in the play where you only listen for several beats—take it in, know what's going on.

NOTE:
Don't Just Sit There

I worry when an actor just sits and reads. Somewhere, some ridiculous teacher said that when they ask you to "read for the role", you just read for the role. There must be some movement, even if it's just a subtle shift. It helps the director to understand your ability to work physically.

NOTE:
Don't Type Yourself Out

Just out of undergrad, fresh to the streets of Gotham, I read a breakdown for a new film being cast: "Seeking young man; early twenty's, brown hair, brown eyes, physically agile with a sense of comedic edge." I ran to that audition. I had this one in the bag. I was all that and more. Didn't I have a fresh BFA in my pocket? Wasn't I considered the best at Emerson College? *Wasn't I the class clown? Was I not great on the tennis court?* As I opened the door to the studio (and what I was sure would be my ticket to fame), I was met with close to two dozen guys who looked exactly like me. I sank into a sweaty depression and immediately lost my nerve. It was a bitter lesson to keep my wits about me and not give over my power. Here's a simple way to hold on to your unique power. For five minutes, study your right hand as if you'd never seen it before. What do you notice? What surprises? What revelations? Now think to yourself: there is no other person who has this hand. You are a uniquely wonderful artist with a secret to share that only you know. I needed that lesson so I share it with you.

On the other hand, if you, (at twenty-three) pursue an audition for a play about seven senior citizens playing gin rummy, you may not make friends of the theatre and the director. It shows a lack of care on your end, and ultimately you have wasted the auditor's time.

NOTE:
At the Call-Back

Play it the way you played it the first time. Unless they give you notes, just remind them why they are giving you a second look. If you got laughs the day before, they might not laugh again. Take heart, the second day is when we need to buckle down and cast this thing. So, don't panic. Just play it with your original choices. They'll let you know if they want you to change your approach. Wear the same clothes for the callback. Just wash them first!

NOTE:
Cold Readings

The director may think you're not right for the role you read for but right for the funny brother. If she asks you to do a cold read, smile, and jump at the chance. That means that instead of having one audition that week, you now have TWO! Take as much time as they will give you to prep. This is where auditions get crazy. And this is the very time you'll be thrilled you read the play! Go out to the waiting room and find as much privacy as possible. Scan the text. Make strong choices and get your head up as much as you can. I have cast dozens of actors from cold reads. It doesn't have to be perfect to be wonderful!

NOTE:
People Business

When I'm casting a show, I often ask myself if I want to be locked in a room with this person for eight hours a day for four weeks? Unless I've been given a star to direct (all bets off) then I'd like to have some affection for my players. Again, none of us are getting rich, so let's at least have a good time. So yes, I think twice about hiring Debbie Downer or Ego Eddie.

I lost a very important job by bad-mouthing the theatre to a complete stranger in the waiting room. I was just cutting up, but I made a crack about the theatre paying so poorly. Ten minutes later, I met that stranger again. He was sitting behind the desk studying my resume. He was the director. So choose wisely where and to whom you complain!

NOTE:
The Monitor

Most auditions have a monitor who facilitates the call for the actors, the room, and the auditors. They will open the room, sign in the actors, collect their resumes, give the auditors a batch of resumes in the proper order, manage the time slots, and answer countless questions. It's a tough job. Crazy, nervous actors, small hallways, and too many appointments. Treat these folks as well as you would the Pope! Insult them and word will get back to the director. At the end of the day, I always ask the monitor if my choice was decent in the waiting room. Also, know that that monitor may currently be an intern but next month they could be a casting assistant and a year from then, a producer. Treat everyone with respect on the way up and on the way down. One never knows.

NOTE:
Perspective

David Cady is a gentleman casting director. Sweet, talented, patient, and supportive. He got his start in the late 70s as an actor in *Merrily We Roll Along* working with Stephen Sondheim and Hal Prince. As a CD, David brought his acting background to all of his casting sessions. Back in the day, I'm sure I auditioned for David close to forty times. Each time, I'd sign in, audition, rush back to my survival gig, and wonder when he'd cast me? It NEVER happened. Never! I got several call-backs but never a booking. If you do the math on subway fare, costumes, pictures and resumes, make-up, and lost work hours, I had hundreds of dollars invested in my relationship with David.

Years later, David and I were both teaching at The American Musical and Dramatic Academy in New York and were catching a coffee between classes in their horrible faculty lounge. There must be some sadistic rule that actors and teachers should be cursed with inhumane conditions. Some of the dirtiest places I've been are green rooms with grease stains from years of actors leaning against the wallpaper! Early on I was in an Off-Broadway show and believed I had made it until I saw that I would be dressing in an abandoned boiler room with heating oil dripping poetically on my make-up table. The worst conditions I ever dealt with was in a little Off-off-Broadway black box theatre where I was performing in a new comedy. We dressed in a public stairwell! (Excuse me, I digress.) Now that I was no longer auditioning for him, I asked David why he continued to call me in for auditions when I never seemed to book. His answer was brilliant and oh so helpful. He said: "I called you in every few weeks because you always read so well, dressed the part, and charmed the producers. You made me look good every time you came in and you were always a choice." WOW! Why did I not know that then? Well, now you do. You can't be everything but you can be a choice.

NOTE:
Understudies

An understudy is an actor who learns one or more roles in a play and is prepared to go on (at a minute's notice) and play the part. If the show has opened, you will have a chance to see it. In that case, your audition must be as close in every way to the actor who is currently playing it. It's an art form to embody someone else's performance. Keep in mind their performance is the direct result of a director's vision. This is no time to get creative. The commercial theatre is a well-oiled machine. The understudy, although crucially important when they do go on, is but a wee cog in the machine. It's a job that requires great initiative and actors of the highest caliber of integrity. No flakes need apply! Make very good friends with everyone, especially the stage managers. They are your friends and your boss. My Off-Broadway debut was in the cast of David Ives' brilliant play of six one-acts, *All in the Timing*. I was taught something right before I went on for *Words, Words, Words* (or the monkey play), by the wonderfully talented and oh-so-generous Danny Burstein. He took me by my shoulders as the scene change music was blaring and my heart was skipping beats and said: "You'll be great, but it's gonna be a lot faster than rehearsal!" My he was right! I don't remember anything about those seven minutes. I was fully out of my body and only years of technique and preparation got me through.

NOTE:
To Laugh or Cry

When I first moved to New York out of undergrad, I, like hundreds of other actors, had no agent, no manager, and no way to get into a legitimate audition for paying gigs. So, open calls were my only alternative. It required getting to the call as early as possible so that I could audition and still make my lunch shift. I had a system. I'd wake up in Brooklyn at 4 a.m., take the train to arrive at the Actors' Equity Center by 4:45 a.m. and set up my little stool, drink my coffee, read *The Post* with fifty other guys and wait until the cranky security guard let us into the building at 8 a.m. In bitter cold and rain some days. One particular cold, rainy March morning, I was bundled up and sitting on my stool at 46th Street off Broadway when a huge truck barreled by splashing about seven gallons of New York's finest sewer water all over me. It was like a Chaplin film without the happy ending. I used the newspaper as a towel, wiped myself dry, finished my coffee, and stayed the course. No one told me about this part of fame. Back in the day, pre-digital days, the casting director took a Polaroid of each actor to attach to their vitals. After I had applied my base and powdered in a filthy hall with twenty other guys dressed like short-order cooks, I lined up for my mug shot. Raising the camera, the CD said "Okay, on three. One, two...". Suddenly, she stopped, lowered the camera, and said with disgust, "Oh Christ! You have the squintiest little eyes; I can barely see them... and three (snap)." An actor has to roll with the cruelty some days. The task is to not let the incivility of the industry pollute your spirit with contempt and doubt. It was very clear to me early on that I was but a wee cog in a huge machine; that I was to hit my mark and not cause trouble. In fact, on my first commercial set, I'll never forget being called to the set and finding five very angry advertising execs sweating and pointing at me. I was to learn later that they were unhappy with me in the principle role. Sure, they had seen seventy actors in three days of auditions and call-backs, but something about my look that day terrified them. The advertising business is a hateful world where fear of failure is the name of the game. So, there I was a young nervous actor dressed in my astronaut outfit wondering why they were grimacing and shaking their fists at me.

"Could he just turn around?"

"Me?

"Yes, could he just turn around?"

"Me?"

"Yes!"

I did. They conferred: "Is there nothing we can do to him? Are we even sure this is the guy we cast? Call the casting office. Check. If it's wrong, can we get that tall guy in time to shoot this?" They were unable to secure their second choice or first. I may have simply been a clerical error, but I shot the spot. Oh, and after seventy minutes of prodding and new shoes, they threw a hat on me (and this was when I still had hair) and suffered my look for the rest of the day! Some days you just don't know whether to laugh or cry.

CONGRATULATIONS!
YOU GOT THE GIG!
The Rules of the Rehearsal Room

NOTE:
Respect

There's nothing in this world quite so awesome and terrifying as stepping into a rehearsal room on the first day of a new project. It's truly awesome! (Okay, I used that word three times now but it truly is!) It's a sacred place where we share our hearts, fears and love with a group of fellow artists. It's a privilege to enter it. As you unearth the humanity of the script and your part, you will discover all of yourself and come close to understanding the meaning of your life, if not its purpose. I've spent forty years there and found myself anew each and every day. I envy you!

NOTE:
The Life of the Room

The actor must know the rules of the rehearsal studio. Understand what they are and why they're there and you'll be fine. Break them, and you'll incur the contempt of the artistic staff and cast and most likely return to your day job.

A rehearsal room can be fraught with insecurity. At some point, we've all dreaded that we'd crash and burn in there and never work again. Certain roles are just so challenging to the soul that the very act of diving into the play can feel harrowing. I directed *A Streetcar Named Desire* with the MFA company at The University of South Carolina. Our Blanche, Yvonne Senat, was up to the challenge, but even this gifted actor was brought to her emotional knees multiple times throughout the grueling five-week schedule, as was I. Classics challenge. When artists put themselves out there, when the truth is sought and fought for, the room is a delicate zone. And it's physically grueling: seven-and a-half hours out of nine hours daily, six days a week. If you're playing someone in emotional straits, you're bound to hit the couch after rehearsal and barely come up for air. In short order, you're dreaming of Ophelia's drowning as if it were your own and calling your therapist. Your job is to remain healthy and be patient. Bring your spirit of openness to the room and trust your director to guide you. In many ways, it's a creative leap of faith. The magnificent producer and director, George C. Wolfe, tells an instructive story about the original production of *Angels in America Part One: Millennium Approaches*. It was a massive hit on Broadway and soon after its opening, the company went back into rehearsal during the day to create *Part Two: Perestroika*, while still playing eight shows a week. Wolfe said that the actors melted down in those rehearsals. It took him a while to understand their fragility. Rehearsals are about doubt, questioning, experimentation. Performance is about confidence and daring. His company became addled because they had to be in both worlds every day. It was just too much. Imagine, you wake up and rehearse from ten to six, desperate to find your character and make sense of the epic that is *Angels in America*. Then you haul ass up to the theatre, catch a quick dinner, take a ten-minute nap in your dressing room (if you're lucky), don your costume, hit the stage running, play a three-hour epic, subway back to Brooklyn, study your lines for tomorrow's rehearsal, black out, wake up, and do it all again. There is only so much space in an actor's head. However, Wolfe and his company figured it out and *Perestroika* was an even bigger hit. Wolfe led his cast to theatrical nirvana. In the process, he came up with the best description of the role of the director in rehearsal: The Designated Driver!

Making art is messy. Stephen Sondheim, the genius composer, said it quite well. The rehearsal process is the art of creating order out of chaos. The room is rife with raw emotions, insecurity and hurt feelings. It's the cost of doing business. A rehearsal room is a very tense place. You'll find directors who make it a safe zone but that may not always happen. Many artists are afraid that they'll be found out as frauds even after a lifetime of good work. Insecurity and genius go hand in hand. It's just one of those paradoxes that you'll find in the business. I know a very talented actor who always believes that she'll be fired after the first table read. It's insane to believe that. It makes no sense. I know that, you know that, but gifted as she is, she still harbors that terror. On the other hand, it keeps her on her toes, and she delivers every time (but the emotional price can be steep). Stay present in the room and keep clear of your head. Leave your fears on the other side of the rehearsal room door and trust your gut. It will never fail you. If you are having a particularly bad day, take a minute to study your palm. That's why you have the job!

The great American painter, Andrew Wyeth, was a child at heart and his lucky kids were blessed by his silliness. He valued play above all else and so their home was full of masks and swords and hats and crazy costumes. Wyeth would regularly thrill his children with fun, imaginative scenarios. He said that creative adults must maintain this sense of play and their inner child. If the rehearsal room is a safe place, a loose room, the creation of a play is joyous. Thrilling. It's this fact that keeps an actor in the game during the rough times. We all know that once cast, the fun begins—right from the first cup of coffee at the table read. The best laughs I've had were in the room and I've witnessed bouts of artistic courage that will stay with me the rest of my life. It really is just like building a fort with the sofa pillows. Oh, there are rough projects, laborious and challenging to the soul, but the joy is in the discovery and that often takes work. But it's not a chore, it's fun. After all, it's called a play!

NOTE:
Directors

Directors don't really care how you get to your performance. Their primary job is to cast well and organize a space where the kids play nice and fulfill their vision of the story. Though not always the norm, it's exhilarating when the director creates a room that is a safe space to explore and create the life of the play. It's the director who sets the tone and creates the atmosphere in which you work. Some directors will try to micromanage your performance. What can I tell you? The industry attracts (and often celebrates) the control freak who can't really be bothered with speaking the language of the classroom. Let's face it, there are numerous acting techniques being espoused in undergraduate programs—too many for any one director to master. With two weeks of rehearsal, five hours a day, time is precious. The director must be free to utilize any imagery she feels will capture the moment, so it's your job to translate direction into something actable. If the direction makes no sense to you, then quietly, at the end of the day, ask for a minute to discuss it with the director. It's the actor's job to do the direction, so clarity is necessary.

In movies and TV, there is often no rehearsal. Stars tend

not to want to rehearse and no one blows out their best work in a camera rehearsal. So, the lowly theatre actor is freaked. I remember playing a big scene in *Law & Order* with Jesse Washington of *Rent* fame, and we never discussed nor rehearsed the four pages. Set up. Shoot it. Thank you. Here, time, budgets, and lights are the problem. You need to get the shot and move on. In the theatre, an actor has some agency. In film, however, (unless you are a commodity like Tom Cruise) you are but a wee cog in the Hollywood sausage factory. Do what you did in the audition. And don't be too interesting. Interesting is for the stars.

Recently, I was discussing the work of a famous young director (DT) with my dear friend and consummate performer John Christopher Jones, an actor who regularly works with said director. I was curious. DT's shows are fascinating, clever, visually stunning. Really good. I wondered, "Just how does he do it?" Christopher remarked that all you need to know is that it's DT's sandbox. Sure, you can make choices as an actor, but just remember it's (DT's) sandbox! Some directors have much of the show already figured out before they even cast the show. (I, by the way, don't. I find it takes all the surprises out of the process and I live for a good mistake!) In this situation, tact is of the utmost importance. If you have a delicate question for the director, speak to her privately. Your artistic frustration, as legit as it may be, could lead to humiliating the director in her sandbox. The great dramatist, John Guare, said that humiliation is modern man's greatest fear. I have been shown up by hostile actors in front of the company, and it's no fun. Remember that the director has a vision but not all the answers. She's rehearsing too. If she changes blocking or the interpretation of the scene, cut her a break. It only means that the story is becoming clearer. A director, like the actor, must have the freedom to change their thinking. The first choice for staging or interpretation is just that, the first. Time and perspective reveal the truth of the story and our first choice can often be weak. Those first choices are usually made under duress. The poor director is thinking, "Oh God, I have to stage this beast brilliantly so the producer thinks I'm doing my job!" The actor is not the only one who is afraid of termination.

Just as each actor works differently, so, too, each director has their own system. It often takes an actor and a director a few days to get in sync. Not to worry. It is always a dance and great dances take a little time.

NOTE:
A Great Class With No Grades

One way to think of rehearsals is that the good ones are just like a class—a great masters level class where the students find the truth in the story through improv, negotiations, sweat, inspiration, and collaboration based on the text. It's why acting is truly a wonderful gig. Every show is an opportunity to learn something new. Robin Williams said that the main reason people go into acting is to become better people. Because of this life-long passion to learn, I find actors to be the most interesting people I have ever met. They are always asking why we behave as we do, and so they learn to ask the right questions and truly listen, and they listen with all of themselves. The rehearsal requires that we bring the Buddhist practice of "beginner's mind" to the table. This is where the ego, the controlling mechanism in our system, gets in the way of creation. The task is to open yourself up to the ghosts in the script. In doing so, the director is not so much a teacher as a facilitator. Great table-work (that portion of the rehearsal process that takes place seated around a table reading and discussing the play) is an intellectual free-for-all where everyone contributes. There are no dumb questions. In fact, it's the simple questions that often bare the greatest results. The inquiry begins to unravel the writing while clarifying the playwright's message. It's thrilling. And it's just the beginning. A week later, the company may find that their original ideas just don't play well on their feet—but it doesn't matter. You need a start; a way in. Moreover, the table helps us all learn how each role fits into the structure. Playwrights don't write plays, they construct them. What part of the building are you? I've seen actors struggle for weeks until they understand what role in the story their character fills. Once that's finalized, the rest of the performance begins to fall into place and becomes fun. Like a good class, we feel intellectually energized by a great rehearsal. The dirty secret is, that frequently, rehearsals are the best part of the job.

NOTE:

Intimacy

For many, risking the truth is the hardest part of acting. Yet there is no art without the risk. And today, the world seems more untrustworthy by the minute. We are in the throes of great change personally and culturally. Actors are more aware of their personal space than ever before, and so love/sex/intimate scenes have taken on a special focus in the rehearsal room or on a Hollywood set. The days of "Just do it" are long over. Now, actors have the right to protect themselves in these situations. This new-found, hard-won privilege has opened up a new position in the room: the Intimacy Coordinator. (IC) The IC works with the actors and the director to help facilitate the staging of scenes with potentially uncomfortable elements—anything from a simple kiss to an all-out assault. She works through every move with the actors so that they feel safe and creative. It's a terrific change and much needed. When you work with an IC, feel free to speak your truth. There is no shame in asking for help or requiring boundaries. The IC will protect you so that you can feel safe to create art without feeling emotionally or physically damaged. Remember, the actor's greatest strength is to say "no." With the advent of the IC, actors are no longer put in positions where they jeopardize their career and reputation by having to say "no." The IC has got your back.

NOTE:

The Rules of the Room

1

If you are not fifteen minutes early,
you are fifteen minutes late.

2

Come prepared to work.

3

Do your period research.

4

Research the script and playwright.

5

Google words and facts you don't know.

6

Come into the room fresh with a free spirit and open attitude.

7

Never walk in front of a director as she is working.

8

If you are playing a comedy or a play with complicated business, get the script out of your hand for the second pass at the scene.

9

Blocking questions? Ask the stage manager after rehearsal. Don't ask the director.

10

Notes are not a personal attack. Take them graciously and work not to get them a second time.

11

Do NOT give notes to a fellow actor. EVER!

12

Study the accent beforehand. You should be able to improvise in the accent not just speak your lines in it.

13

Learn your words letter-perfect.

14

Respect the backstage artisans and crew.

15

Learn the technicians' names!

16

Personal problem? Reach out to stage management.

17

In technical rehearsals, don't carry on so that the designers can't concentrate on their work.

18
Take care of personal hygiene.
Don't smoke before a love scene.

19
Don't sit in the room playing with your phone.
It sends the wrong message. Pun intended.

20
Keep chatter to a minimum.

21
Lateness: I directed a very surly student actor who made a habit of coming late to rehearsal. Once can be forgiven but repeated lateness is grounds for dismissal. If you do come late, you MUST apologize to everyone. You must. Do the math. If there are eight people working on a play and you are ten minutes late, that's eighty minutes of wasted rehearsal. Needless to say, Mr. Grumpy Pants could not find it in himself to offer an apology. As my British friends would say, "That's just not ON!"

22
Study the director. Chances are you will become a director at some point, and you may learn something.
(I wish I had done more of this earlier on!)

23
Study the floor plan. Pay attention to the tape. Close non-existent doors. Walk up steps. You are building muscle memory. It makes the transition to the stage easier.

24
Come prepared to work.

25
Tip your dresser.

26
If you are in the first scene, be backstage and prepared ten minutes before curtain.

27
Speak the correct cues to your fellow actors. Don't be that actor who loses a laugh by sending the wrong cue.

28
In dress rehearsals, study the sound cues, costumes, set pieces and lighting—all the new elements. Allow the work of the designers to influence your final choices. Yes, you know your character better than anyone, but they know the world of the play.

29
Write thank you cards. To ALL the players.

30
Work in rehearsal (not final) costumes as soon as possible.

31
Work with props as soon as possible.

32
NEVER say, "Is this what we are using?" about a rehearsal prop. It's just rude and you will make yourself look really bad. Final props usually arrive when you move from the rehearsal room to the stage.

33
Something doesn't have to be perfect to be wonderful. In fact, striving for perfection in an art form that celebrates humanity misses the point entirely.

34
It's not all about you.

35
When in doubt, call a friend and complain to them.

36
Clean up after yourself.

37
"Showmances" (affairs made in rehearsal, usually between actors) are dangerous. Just wait a few weeks!

38
Eat properly for energy and stay hydrated.

39
Watch the other actors in rehearsal. Their work may tell you a lot about the play's focus, style, and pace.

40
Be the kind of person you'd want to do a show with.

41
The actress Ethel Merman used to say, "Don't do your homework in rehearsal and don't rehearse in performance."

NOTE:
Notes

When the director gives a note, write it down. Review it and incorporate it into your next rehearsal. Give the director the chance to see if the note helps before you question it. I worked with a thirty-year-old graduate student in a very reputable graduate program who believed that my notes to her were a personal attack on her talent. Many times, she'd take the first note then, after my second observation, roll her eyes, close her notebook, and take out her phone for the rest of the session. Sadly, she was a student and could not be fired. She spent a good deal of rehearsal intimidating me. I wanted to say, "Please, don't intimidate me. If you do, I won't be able to help you." Notes mean the director is seeing the possibilities in your performance. When I say nothing to you, it's probably because you are not giving me anything to help. On the other hand, if you're brilliant and clearly moving in the direction I imagined for the part, I might not say much other than to acknowledge that you are on track.

ARTISTIC HEALTH
Take Good Care of Yourself

NOTE:

Life Coaching

"Intention" is often a word used in acting class but it has another meaning in the business. Intention. What do you want to create? What do you intend to do? What do you see yourself doing in five years? Intentionality. My career coach, the brilliant Madeleine Homan Blanchard, always says, "This or something better!" There is no "something better" if you're not working toward a clear, viable goal: a movie role with Brad Pitt as your father; the next lead in an Elton John musical for Disney; voicing a Pixar character in the next *Toy Story* sequel opposite Tom Hanks. It matters not if these goals are attained, but the energy that intentionality brings to your daily life and career is immeasurable. You must not wait around for someone to offer you your ticket in. It does NOT work that way. I know scores of gifted artists that are selling insurance in South Dakota now because they entrusted their career to others and failed to embrace intentionality. Don't kid yourself, your work does not end because you landed an agent. After the initial high of signing a two-year contract for representation, I recommend getting your ass out of that office and making your own work and building contacts. See it, plan it and execute it. Your intention will attract fascinating people who will take the journey with you.

NOTE:
Save Your Soul

If theatre emerged from storytelling and ritual, then acting is a cultural ministry. We don't act to please ourselves. It is an art form based on serving our fellow man. Whether on stage or on camera, our focus is on the other. In a scene, our primary focus is affecting our scene partner and ultimately changing the audience. Your artistic truth actively heals the audience. Your emotional courage guides the audience to a higher spiritual plain and this act of service is, in itself, a spiritual act. Theatre, in particular, is a redemptive art. Until the closing show, actors are given a second chance to redeem their performance, to strive ever closer to truth. By keeping your focus on service, you leave your ego behind and that's always a good thing.

There is also a religious-like ritual in preparing for a live performance that is both necessary and centering. At 7:30, half hour is called by stage management and the company assembles to prepare for the evening's show. Coffee, vocal and physical warm-ups, make-up, prop check, reviewing your lines, a moment's meditation, a prayer to the theatre gods, and you're off to the stage. Ritual creates a sense of expectancy and puts you in a state of readiness to connect with the text, the character, the situation, and the audience. Like everything in this book, rituals are very personal and as you grow, you will create your own. Most importantly, rituals and this time before performance MUST be respected.

When I was a graduate student at The Alabama Shakespeare Festival, I had a small role, Francisco, in *The Tempest*. I had exactly fourteen lines but they were pure exposition (background information) so they were critically important. I was lucky to have the role as the MFA company rarely got lines in the professional shows. I should have been grateful. But at twenty-five, cocky and oh so casual, I spent half-hour joking around and throwing a baseball in the green room garden with my buddies. It was a Saturday matinée, and I was having a grand old time doing anything but warming up. I made my entrance, heard my cue and totally dried up. I couldn't think of a single word. My stuttering and fumbling had nothing to do with the play. It was a horrible moment that proved that I was a rookie, an amateur, and worse, I put the storytelling in jeopardy and made my cast-mates look like idiots. How was the audience to know that Ferdinand may be alive if I didn't say the lines? Not from me. I was humiliated. I left the stage and headed to my dressing room to hide. However, on the way, the senior character man, the lovely and oh-so-gentle David O. Petersen (who was the focus of my fourteen lines), stopped me in the hall. I made a joke and then David slapped me hard across the face. All he said was, "Don't mess with this show. Show some damn respect." I had failed to respect half-hour. That thirty minutes of precious transition from the civilian world to the world of the play? Without it, you're just pretending to be an actor.

NOTE:
Therapy

I highly recommend therapy! It's our job to ask "why." Why does Blanche's obsession to be admired lead her to sleep with dozens of lovers? What makes *Iron Man* tick? So, it follows that we must ask why we do what we do, choose whom we choose, study what we study? Why are we pursuing this madness? Sure, you can reach out to your minister, but do you really want to tell your deepest fantasies to Pastor Jerry when you know that in a few minutes he'll be seated next to you and your mom at the mother and son pancake breakfast? No, dammit! Instead, get thee to a therapist or at least a counselor. Do the digging. Unearth the bones in your family. Create your own myths. Get to the bottom of it all. There is no downside. And if school provides it for free, go twice a week. Mental health is as important as physical and vocal health and just as necessary to a long career if not more so. Understanding yourself is a life-long process and that exploration will inform your work as an actor.

NOTE:
Pride & Humility

As you hustle for work, you must have a strong backbone to handle the myriad rejections that come with show business. At the same time, you must maintain an openness in the rehearsal room so that you can bring your heart to the process. As an actor, your job requires equal parts pride and humility. It's a daily balancing act.

NOTE:
Miles

When I'm struggling in the room as an actor or director, I'm comforted by the great trumpeter, Miles Davis. Early in his career, he was working with Charlie Parker. On one particular set of solos, Miles let Parker solo for nearly thirty minutes. Even by jazz standards, that's a long time. When asked after the gig why he let Parker go on so long, Miles replied: "The brother was searching for something." That's true for all of us.

NOTE:
Jessy

Botanists have discovered that trees have an advanced underground communication system among them that helps them grow and allows them to fortify other trees in their forest. Not surprisingly, when a tree is cut down, everything around it suffers great change. Some plants thrive while others die. That was the crisis I faced twenty years ago. In 2003, my sweet, remarkable six-year-old son, Jess Ilias, suddenly died. The details don't help. I wrestled with the universe. How could Jay not be sleeping in his room, making theatre, and keeping our family in stitches? There was not a lot of solace to go around in those dark hours, but one thing fortified my spirit. Jessy was a brilliant actor, best I've ever known.

It was pure delight to behold his acting and he loved that his daddy was an actor and a director. But our tree (albeit, quite skinny and not very tall) was no longer alive in our house and his mother and I had to decide to give up or go on. It was nearly a year after he passed that I found myself in a forest... alone. I took an oath that I would honor Jessy by continuing to work in the theatre, and I have ever since. Never looked back. Not all you good readers have such dramatic stories behind you, but I know that all of you need to make a choice and find a solid, spiritually-based reason to press on and play this challenging game. Jess was mine. I ask you to consider yours.

NOTE:

The Last Act

Many of life's failures are people who did not realize how close they were to success when they gave up. Steve Jobs sheds light. He is quoted as saying, "… you can't connect the dots looking forward, you can only connect them looking backward. So, you have to trust the dots will connect in your future." Commencement address at Stanford University, June 12, 2005.

When in doubt, go back to your trusty palm. Study your hand. There is no other like it in the universe. It is the source of your art, your story, your character. You will be tested but don't let your fears overwhelm your desires, your dreams. The acting profession is a wonderful way to live one's life. Tom Hanks said it well: "If you love what you do for a living, you'll never have to work another day in your life!" Build your craft, embrace the world, cherish your heart, love your friends and trust these words: You are enough.

NOTE:

Avanti!

CURTAIN CALL
Resources for Actors

Actors' Equity Association
Actorsequity.org
165 W 46th St. # 15,
New York, New York 10036
(212) 869-8530
Equity Membership Candidacy
https://www.actorsequity.org/join/emc/

Screen Actors Guild/American Federation of Television and Radio Artists
Sagaftra.org
1900 Broadway 5th floor,
New York, New York 10023
(212) 827-1401

Publications (guide to agents, managers, and casting directors)
Backstage
www.backstage.com
Playbill
https://www.playbill.com

Research (a recommended reading list and other resources for actors)

Freeing the Natural Voice: Imagery and Art in the Practice of Voice and Language, by Kristin Linklater
www.linklatervoice.com

A Dream of Passion, by Lee Strasberg

Respect for Acting, by Uta Hagen

The Actor's Art and Craft, by William Esper and Damon DiMarco

An Actor Prepares, by Constantin Stanislavsky

On the Technique of Acting, by Michael Chekhov

Acting in Commercials: A Guide to Auditioning and Performing on Camera, by Joan See

Caryn West
theauditioncoach.com

Intimacy Coordinator
intimacycoordinator.com

Printed in the USA
CPSIA information can be obtained
at www.ICGtesting.com
LVHW041907230824
789115LV00005B/42